NetSuccess:
How Real Estate Agents
Use the Internet

NetSuccess:

How

Real Estate Agents

Use the

Internet

Scott Kersnar

NetSuccess: How Real Estate Agents Use the Internet
First Edition
by Scott Kersnar

Published by Songline Studios, Inc.
101 Morris Street, Sebastopol, CA 95472

Editors: Stephen Pizzo and Melissa Koch

Printing History: August 1996:   First Edition

Songline Guides is a trademark of Songline Studios, Inc.

 This book is printed on acid-free paper with 85% recycled content, 15% post-consumer waste. The publishers are committed to using paper with the highest recycled content available consistent with high quality.

ISBN: 1-56592-213-1

Cover Design by Edie Freedman

Contents

About the Author

Scott Kersnar is a freelance author and consultant. His byline appears regularly in the National Mortgage News, a publication that covers the residential mortgage markets. Scott has been a newpaper publisher and editor and an active real estate broker. He has authored award-winning neighborhood disaster preparedness materials and taught junior college real estate courses. A former English teacher, Scott holds a master's degree from Stanford University. He and his wife Darlene enjoy life on 72 secluded acres in Northern California's redwood country. Scott can be reached at *skersnar@wco.com.*

Acknowledgments

I most want to thank the working real estate professionals whose stories and accumulated wisdom grace these pages. I of course want to thank my editors, Stephen Pizzo and Melissa Koch without whose guidance and collaboration this book would not have been possible. I am deeply grateful to my wife Darlene for her encouragement and patience when deadline pressures grew intense.

Scott Kersnar

Introduction: All Roads Can Lead to You

You picked up this book, so you've obviously noticed the Internet (also known as the Net) playing an increasing role in the real estate business. Some of your competitors already have home pages on the Net. Not only that, out-of-town buyers have started asking you to email them your new listings.

Clearly, you've put this off as long as you can.

- ▶ It's Not Just About Computers
- ▶ The Virtual Real Estate Office
- ▶ How to Use *NetSuccess*

RELAX!

If this is your introduction to using the Internet, don't worry. You're certainly not alone. A remarkable number of real estate agents still have no presence on the Net.

Why not?

Consultant Mary Kay Aufrance believes many agents fear that widespread public access to online listings and for-sale-by-owner home pages heralds doomsday for the traditional real estate business and their own careers:

CONTACT

Tom & Mary Kay Aufrance
Aufrance Associates
http://www.highsierra.com
tmaufr@highsierra.com

Mary Kay Aufrance

> There is a lot of fear on the part of many individuals about their roles in real estate changing or being eliminated by the Internet. I think the fear of being wiped out by agents who use the Internet is felt most by those who haven't yet taken even the first baby step into using computers.

Mary Kay and her husband Tom teach seminars for real estate agents interested in learning how to use the Internet. Some who take their classes are skeptical:

> We get students asking us, "But does anybody really *buy* a home on the Internet?" We tell them that the listings and the advertising are just the tip of the iceberg. Once they've gotten into it, the overwhelming attitude of all the real estate agents has always been a feeling of control and success.

PERSONAL ACCOUNT

Michael Russer
Russer Communications
mrusser@quadran.com

It's Not Just About Computers

Michael Russer, who teaches Internet seminars for real estate agents across the country, says:

> Fifty years from now, historians will look back on our time and society, shake their collective heads and say, "My God, what incredible changes those people must have gone through!" Those of us in the real estate industry, however, are likely to look back in similar amazement in just two to five years. There is no question that the Internet serves as fuel for much of this accelerating change. Unfortunately, far too many people equate the Internet with computers, and thereby miss the point. It is no more about computers than traveling is about trains, boats, or planes. It is about people connecting with people in ways that we can barely begin to imagine.
>
> Far beyond just another way of communicating, the Internet represents a fundamental shift in the way people all over the world will relate with each other. Real estate agents who strive to understand and apply the Internet on this richer, deeper level will be amply rewarded not only with a far superior means of doing real estate, but with a much more empowering way to connect and deal with people as well.

WHY MAKE ALL THAT DUST?

A skeptical broker I know stayed suspicious for a long time about computers. Even after he computerized his office he viewed the Net as a diversion for his sales staff, and certainly not a sales tool. All he could see in his mind's eye was his salespeople staring slack jawed at their monitor screens instead of drumming up listings and sales. That image violated his old-school maxims that "the office is a tomb" and "losers mind the office while go-getters go and get."

It came to pass (as they say in stories about people who experience miraculous conversions) that one day this particular broker looked over the shoulder of one of his computer-transfixed salespeople, and what he saw changed his mind on the spot. Instead of a computer game or a tour of one of those "exotic" World Wide Web sites, what he saw was strictly business email bringing his salesperson a hefty out-of-state referral.

He watched his agent click the reply button to send back a referral agreement and then proceed to take the prospect's email address and send along initial relocation information the agent kept ready in a computer file. Blip, done. Just like that.

That skeptical broker learned very quickly how to send and receive email and do a lot of other things he never thought he'd do. Now he's not as anxious to have his agents out of the office at "business lunches," leaving their business cards with the bartenders or racing to see a new listing before anyone else in the office gets there. Those things are still important, but why make all that dust if you can also spend your time wisely prospecting at your computer?

Of course if you have a laptop (with modem) and a cellular phone, your office can always be with you. When you're out on a listing interview, a laptop and an Internet connection let you show comparable properties in your Web site (or those of other agents) to help your owners better understand the market they face. You can work some days in the office and some days at home. Telecommuting means never having to call in sick.

CAN YOU AFFORD NOT TO BE ON THE WORLD WIDE WEB?

As 1995 drew to a close, there were more than 40 million American households with personal computers and an estimated 30 million people using the Internet. Approximately 90 million people around the globe were using email in one form or another. With that many people either connected or with the capability of going online whenever they decide to do it, can you afford not to be accessible on the

Net any more than you could afford not to be reachable by phone? The answer is no. You can't.

Real estate has always been among the most competitive of professions, where the slightest advantage can make the difference between winning and losing. So the next time a homeowner asks, "Can you post a picture of my home on your Web site?" will you be able to smile and say yes?

Will buyers find you or your listings if they begin their search for a new home—as many now do—on the Internet rather than checking the newspaper or going from real estate office to real estate office? Will your Web page be there to help guide them to the home of their dreams?

Don't stand idly by while hot prospects visit real estate home pages belonging to other agents. You want to be the agent receiving email descriptions from those prospects outlining their real estate wants and needs.

Internet-connected agents draw customers. And not just run-of-the-mill customers. Demographic studies by O'Reilly and Associates and others show that the bulk of Internet users are 35 to 50 years old and earn $50,000 a year or more. Internet home shoppers are educated, affluent and informed. If they send an email query during a home page visit, that contact can be worth dozens of cold calls or prospecting letters.

These people are motivated and qualified. Transferring executives, engineers, couples looking for a second home…that's the kind of lucrative business you'll be missing.

I'm not making a sales pitch for the Internet. Recall, though, that we have seen the real estate business embrace new technology in the past that was supposed to revolutionize the business but didn't. Remember when multiple listing services first went online with those little terminals? That was less than twenty years ago. In reality, online MLS didn't really do much to change the real estate business. It just made it cheaper and faster for offices to get the latest listings to collect comparable-sales data for a competitive market analysis. However, mistaking the Internet for just another marginal technological change would be a gross error.

The real estate agents interviewed for this book already embrace this new tool and have compelling stories to tell. In the pages ahead, you will hear those stories in their own words. What you will learn is that the Internet is not a magic wand. It won't make a bad salesperson into a million-dollar-a-year agent. Instead, it is a powerful communication tool that will let already good agents and productive offices leverage their existing strengths in ways they never dreamed possible.

REAL ESTATE IN THE GLOBAL VILLAGE

In a January 1996 speech to bankers, U.S. Comptroller of the Currency Eugene Ludwig quoted estimates that there will be 200 million Internet users by the year 2000 and $3 trillion worth of electronic commerce by 2005. By 2010, up to 55 percent of shopping by Americans will be conducted online.

Being connected to the Web cannot help but broaden your perspective on how you do business. Many already find the Internet an essential tool in getting referrals and enquiries from distant communities.

In the pages ahead you will meet agents who are baiting their Web hooks to snare overseas investors looking for bargains and security in U.S. real estate. As Asia begins to replace Europe as the source of most U.S. immigration and investment, some agents are tuning their home pages to attract real estate shoppers from Hong Kong and Taiwan to capitalize on the uncertain economic and political futures of those two currently affluent markets.

The Web venue is made to order for those agents who—themselves recent immigrants to the U.S.—still have family and other contacts back in their home countries and can help bridge the move for those who want to follow. The Net gives them an effective way to advertise their properties and services back home, using their native languages, with deference to ethnic customs and a unique understanding of the financial and cultural problems immigrants must overcome.

Other real estate agents aim exclusively at worldwide commercial real estate customers, broadening the pool of potential investors for multimillion dollar hotels, shopping centers and office buildings by exposing those properties to a worldwide market. Where international newspaper advertising rates may have been prohibitively expensive before, now—for as little as $25 a month—a Web site allows anyone with a computer and modem to reach a worldwide market. Compare that with the price of a single small ad in the Asian edition of the *Wall Street Journal*!

To all but a very few agents, the globalization of real estate sales may not be important. But for those who do decide to carve themselves an international niche, the opportunities will only grow in the years ahead, with the Internet a major factor in that growth.

But this book is not about practicing electronic real estate far from home. Here is an excerpt from an email message a real estate agent sent me six months after creating his Web page. The message is one to take to heart:

> My partner and I are responsible for bringing the WWW [World Wide Web] to this small Arkansas town about 12 miles from Clinton's Whitewater property. The impact our page has had in this area is most astounding.
>
> As you probably are aware, the biggest demographic change taking place in America today is the widespread move back to small towns. A Web site, in my opinion, is essential for attracting people to a small town. However, the content must be right!
>
> Our page is being hit several thousands of times per week. I get good buyer leads weekly. In fact I get more by Web than any other way.
>
> Gary R. Cooley, Realtor

Hit
The smallest unit of visitor access to a Web page. 10 to 12 hits is one widely acccepted minimum measure of an actual single visit.

THE VIRTUAL REAL ESTATE OFFICE

The electronic world created by the Internet and other media is often called virtual reality. The virtual world can be a powerful servant. Once you join that world by investing in a computer and modem, thinking of your virtual office as just a technologically souped-up version of your current operation is to embrace only a small part of the real potential within your grasp. As we will see later, a virtual real estate operation promises to give you control of your customers from first contact through closing, and to create entirely new income streams as well.

A well-equipped virtual office would not only have its own Web pages and email, but would give you tools to build alliances with other businesses in the real estate food chain. You know who these businesses are because you already refer customers to them every day: title, mortgage and insurance companies, as well as appraisers, home inspectors, and pest control companies.

Until now, even though they represent the first link in that chain, agents were forced to send their customers elsewhere to secure their insurance and mortgages when a sale was made. This not only meant sending that valuable business to others without compensation, it meant losing control of the customer and the aspects of the transaction those third parties handled.

Robert Moles, president of Contempo Realty in California's Silicon Valley, says that because the 12 or 13 percent of a real estate transaction that goes to fees is increasingly under attack in today's competitive marketplace, it has become crucial for real estate brokerages to offer bundled services at the point of sale.

To meet that challenge, "connected" real estate companies are building within their operations value added networks or VANs. These are alliances with online companies that provide the services needed to get a home sold, inspected, financed and insured. Agents can now sit customers down in front of the same computer that maintains their Web pages and connect those customers directly to lenders offering mortgage loans. Using videoconferencing, a loan application can be filled out online and approval granted in minutes. Next, the title process can be initiated, the appraisal ordered, home inspectors and insurers contacted, all without homebuyers having to leave their agent's office, all initiated at a single point of sale.

We'll look at some VANs, commercial services and ad hoc associations. Evolving changes in the Real Estate Settlement Procedures Act are expected to make it easier for real estate brokers to receive compensation when one of their buyers or sellers does business with a VAN member.

Failing to grasp the resulting opportunities will put you at a disadvantage in at least two ways. First, your customers will be deprived of the convenience such VANs offer. Not having to run all over town to find insurance or a loan is no small matter from the customer's perspective. Second, not being involved in a VAN can mean real estate offices suffer loss of referral income that competitors will gladly pocket.

AT THE CROSSROADS

So here you are, at the crossroads, ready to take the next step. It's really not a very large step. After all, you don't need much to get started building a Web site: a computer, a $150 modem, less than $50 worth

FIGURE INTRO-1
*Contempo Realty's home page
(http://www.contempo.com/
Donf@coastaihomes.com)*

of software, and \$15 to \$25 a month for an Internet connection. In all, a total investment of less than \$1,500 could do the job.

But you may have heard the same spiels for the Net that you heard when you bought those business cards with your picture on them, or the keychains and refrigerator magnets sporting your logo, or the pictures of your listings on late night TV, or the ads (again featuring your face) on the supermarket shopping carts. Every one of these promotional gimmicks had "a proven track record." Each of those sales aids cost you money and promised to "pay for itself many times over if you close one small sale or get one good listing."

Before you decide the Internet is just another sales gimmick, pay attention to some of the most successful practitioners of real estate on the Net—like the midwestern agent we tried to interview who asked not to be mentioned in this book because he didn't want to lose his competitive advantage over sleepier local competitors.

SELLERS EXPECT TO FIND YOU ON THE WEB

More and more sellers in communities large and small have heard about the Web and expect you to be there. But the "build it and they will come" philosophy of home page development will not work. You can't just slap a Web page up and leave it dangling unattended like a piece of flypaper. Nothing will say more about your business and how you run it than how you engineer your home page. Some of the agents featured in this book learned this lesson the hard way; through trial and error they've developed a home page chemistry that works to produce leads and business.

What is it that customers want when they come to a real estate agent's page? What do they need? The Internet is still largely virgin territory for marketing. The Net itself and its users' needs, wants, likes and dislikes change quickly. But some fundamental dos and don'ts are beginning to emerge. You can learn them here from the real estate agents who are pioneers in this new territory.

HOW TO USE *NETSUCCESS*

This book is designed to do five things for you:

- Ease you into using the communication tools related to the Internet
- Show you how successful agents use the Net and the World Wide Web to build business

- Show you how to harness the Net to give you greater control over your own real estate career

- Give you a quick opportunity to immerse yourself in the Internet world many of your customers and competitors already know well

- Help you create the kind of effective Web presence that can bring you so much business you'll consider hiring an assistant. Or more than one.

The first thing we'll do is introduce you to email, the primary online tool, and take a first quick look at the wealth of resources on the World Wide Web. In Chapters 2 and 3 we'll discuss getting connected to the Internet and take a closer look at real estate tools the Internet offers. These chapters are ones you'll come back to for crucial information.

In Chapter 4 we'll take a look at some successful real estate Web sites and what makes them work. We'll hear what the owners of those sites have to say about how they created their pages and what they learned along the way.

Chapter 5 will discuss the gear of the telecommuting real estate agent. We'll see how being connected can liberate you from the limitations of time and place. We will look at a day in the life of some telecommuting agents to show what changes and what stays the same when you make technology a full partner in your working life.

Chapter 6 will show how you can teach your customers to "shop you" online so they will come back when they're ready to buy a home.

Chapter 7 will debate whether you should build your own Web site or take advantage of the multiplicity of service providers ready to help you. Chapter 8 will be devoted to the business of linking your Web site to others. The prettiest, most interactive page in the world won't do you any good if people can't find it easily.

Once you've looked at the choices open to you, Chapter 9 will offer the important chance to sit down and write a Web site business plan. What do you expect to achieve? Where do you spend? Do you do it all at once or one step at time? How do you create a niche for yourself? The prospect of putting a version of yourself out on the Web offers a perfect time to take a look at your goals.

Chapter 10 will look at industry forces and market networks to consider which ones have the staying power and reach to help you make sales. As players change and new ones come online, you need to find out what connections can be expected to work for you. How can you establish a Web presence that will stand you in good stead no matter how things change? You'll hear some good news about the future for agents.

Chapter 11 will look at how the Web is affecting commercial real estate, REITs, exchangers and lenders. Seeing the way they use the Web will offer you valuable perspectives and options.

What will be the next big technological marvel to unfold? Every book about the Net is likely to have a chapter taking some wild stabs at predicting the future. Chapter 12 is ours, and the experts and veterans offering their thoughts here have been watching this thing evolve for a long time—and shaping it as well.

I Extend Your Reach

The changing face of real estate communications can be seen best on the face of our business cards. Increasingly, agents' cards offer a choice of communication options: phone, pager, fax, and now, email and their URL.

Before we jump into the "how tos" of getting connected and using the Internet, let's pause a moment in this chapter to explore a couple of the "whys" of getting connected. Nothing you can do will give you a greater return for the money you spend than the money you spend on an Internet connection. Nothing.

▶ Email: The Shortest Distance Between Two Points

▶ What's Out There? A Wealth of Web Resources

EMAIL: THE SHORTEST DISTANCE BETWEEN TWO POINTS

Not long ago when personal fax machines became available, many of us saw no need for the gadgets. We'd become so accustomed to either settling for the U.S. mail, when a day or two didn't seem to matter—or to jumping in our car and driving 100 miles to hand-deliver documents for signature when it did—that the fax machine's immediacy didn't seem important. Then one by one our competitors started using fax machines, and we found out that fewer and fewer of the people we did business with were willing to wait even minutes for the documents they felt they needed now. Soon the question "What's your fax number?" became a refrain we heard many times a day, until we each bit the bullet, bought a fax, and found it an indispensable tool.

Today we have email. Understanding the power of email comes with its first use. After months of harping, I finally convinced a broker friend to start putting his email address on his promotional materials. He had an America Online account, but had never used his email. I kept telling him that he was missing a tremendous networking and communications opportunity, not to mention a wonderfully personal way to stay in touch with clients. Then one morning I opened my own email and found this note:

> Scott, good morning!
>
> Hey, this really works. I am no longer an email virgin. You really know how to get my heart pumping. When I got a call from Chris Smith the other day, I didn't even know my email address when he asked. But when he said "referral," and "$400,000," I said I better get to know what's happening here. So Susan in my office helped me with my first email to him. I want to tell you, Scott, that I really appreciate all the help you have given to me. And please keep riding me. I need all the punch you can give me.

Electronic mail (email) is an immediate benefit. When you get your Internet connection, you get an email address along with it. Nothing more to buy. It simply comes along with the package, just as your street address does when you move to a new house. Once you have your own email address, you can email anyone else who has one, too, and vice versa. Cost? Zero. Delivery speed? The speed of light.

Email lets you:

- Communicate easily with buyers. For those still looking, you can email them new listings without concern about time of day or whether they are at work or home. You send the email off and they pick it up at their convenience. You can even attach photos of properties.

- Soothe sellers who get nervous when their listing doesn't move. Email is a great way to let them know about market activity, recent sales, and showings that may have taken place when they were not home. Sending sellers email updates once a week is a good way to keep them involved and informed.

- Keep on top of service providers like title companies, lenders, and appraisers. Email reminders help speed up delivery of services. The ability to order and receive a pest control inspection via email can cut what is often a ten-day wait down to a day or two. And when that report arrives, forwarding a copy of it to buyer and seller can be just a mouse click away.

- Send lenders and title companies needed documentation. Reducing some of that from paper to digital form is all well and good, but if you can't deliver the digital documents, you're back to square one. You can send an entire file via email.

Quite simply, email has become a powerful new tool for real estate agents. Those who use it and use it wisely will find that it extends their reach, allows them to leverage existing office resources beyond anything they imagined possible, and adds a dynamic dimension to their work that can only be fully understood over time.

Having email also allows you access to the growing number of professional Internet mailing lists (also known as listservs). A mailing list allows a group of people with common interests to exchange messages on that topic. When you send mail to the list, everyone who is subscribed to the list sees your mail.

Those real estate agents who have already integrated email into their operations will be the first to sing its praises. Some sound almost evangelical.

PERSONAL ACCOUNT

**Ira and Carol Serkes,
CRS, GRI
Berkeley RE/MAX Realtor**
*http://www.home-buy-sell.
com/Realtor*

*Realtor@home-buy-
sell.com*

Effective use of email

Realtors Ira and Carol Serkes of Berkeley, California, were early Internet adopters. Keeping abreast of technological change has become a habit with them, not a chore. And they mince no words with those who whine about the learning curve. I made the mistake one day of grumbling about having to master a piece of Web-related software. Ira snapped, "Get used to it. It never stops." Here's a sample of the Serkes' take on email.

You'll use email for more than just sending messages to your friends and clients. We sold one of our listings using email. We'd been in the counteroffer stage, and I couldn't reach the seller because his phone was always busy. It turns out his son was surfing the Net! I got his son's email address, typed up the counteroffer, emailed it to the seller, and told him to email me his approval. We followed up with the original documents via snail mail (the post office).

You can even send email to a client who doesn't have a computer! For a nominal charge, CompuServe will convert your email message to a fax and transmit it to a fax machine.

One agent I know scanned property management reports for a client who lived in Hong Kong. He sent the client an email message, and electronically attached the reports. It cost him pennies to send the document (our cost is about one cent for two minutes of connect time) vs. $10 or more for courier service. His client received the documents instantaneously!

EMAIL ADDRESSES FOR EVERYONE IN THE OFFICE

As with the fax, you will find a multitude of uses for email as you integrate it into your business. But to unlock the full promise of email in your real estate office, every sales associate should have his or her own email address. This is a requirement, not an option.

That's right: an email address for every member of your office.

FIGURE 1-1
*Ira and Carol Serkes' home page
(http://www.home.buy.sell.com/
Realtor/
Realtor@home.buy.sell.com)*

The reason I mention this so forcefully is that otherwise it's likely to be ignored. This is largely due to the fact that the real estate profession has had a haphazard relationship with the personal computer. PCs have tended to arrive in real estate offices one by one in a sporadic manner. Rarely does an office go electronic in one fell (and costly) swoop. Some broker-managers, perhaps because the first computer and modem to arrive in the office belonged to one of the salespeople, have not explored the highest and best use of email because they understand that it would require a PC on every desk and a small local network—in other words, a capital investment they would prefer to stave off for as long as possible.

So when some brokers get the urge to tap into the advantages of email, they try to do so on the cheap by having everyone's email channeled through a single company "postmaster" who downloads and distributes email as time and the press of other business permit. This practice defeats the unique elements that make email such an efficient and powerful communications tool.

EMAIL LETS YOU LEVERAGE YOUR TIME

One of the great advantages email offers is its 24-hour-a-day there-when-you-want-it nature. I check my email ten times a day. I want my email fresh. And I want the ability to respond directly and immediately to the sender. I don't want anyone else downloading stuff for me.

During a given day I may get a query from someone and respond immediately. My response may be incomplete and that person may re-respond, asking the question in greater depth. I may respond again to supply requested details or seek clarification. This tennis match may go on for five or six back-and-forths before the question is answered or the problem resolved. It's a bit like being in a meeting with the other person even though she might be hundreds of miles away.

Moreover, while this virtual email meeting is going on, we're both busy taking phone calls and doing other things between exchanges. There are times when I have several of these conversations going on at once. Talk about maximizing your time!

An important point: email messages are like casual conversation. When you have a dozen or so messages in your mailbox, you deal with them quickly. Most of the time you type a short response and shoot it back, typos and all. Seldom do you sit there crafting sentences and rewriting them into a piece of formal correspondence before sending it off.

Besides your thoughts you can also attach to your email full documents or digitized photos of your latest listings. Email is about communication that is fast, efficient, and ridiculously inexpensive.

All the agents interviewed for this book agreed that email has become the most essential tool in their electronic toolbox, and the tool they use most often. They shake their heads in bewilderment when they see the stubborn holdouts among their peers resisting the point. "I thought agents understood the 'you snooze, you lose' rule of sales, but when it comes to computers and email, many agents still lag way behind the learning curve," said one observer.

There are many faces and uses for email. The ability to use email for daily correspondence and as a point of initial contact with prospects is essential. You simply don't have the option to ignore this tool.

Once you have taken a more detailed look at getting connected to the Internet in Chapter 2 and at using email in Chapter 3, and you have an email address, let me know how you like it. Just email me at *realestate@songline.com*.

WHAT'S OUT THERE?
A WEALTH OF
WEB RESOURCES

Email is one communication tool available to real estate agents. The World Wide Web, which we'll describe in greater detail in Chapter 3, is another way for you to communicate with potential clients and find valuable resources for your business. With its ability to display text and graphics and link to various resources for your clients, the Web allows you to show real estate without depleting your gas tank. The Web also offers a bottomless pit of resources real estate agents can tap into. In fact, the real estate business is so perfectly suited to the Web that real estate-related sites are multiplying (and improving in quality) with each passing day. For example, as this book went to press, the National Association of Realtors Web site (*http://www. realtor.com*) was reporting more hits per month than any other commercial site we know of.

Once you're able to view Web pages on your computer, the World Wide Web will give you answers to almost any question you could imagine about real estate, loan products, marketing techniques, Web publishing itself, and so on, ad infinitum. Think of the Web as the biggest library in the world where you need only state the subject and the answers are served up in seconds.

FIGURE 1-2

The National Association of Realtors home page (http://www.realtor.com email: ebeckman@realtor.com)

PERSONAL ACCOUNT

Becky Swann
IRED
http://www.ired.com
becky@onramp.com

CONTACT

Brad Inman
Inman News Features
http://www.inman.com
InmanNews@aol.com

A Road Map

Internet Real Estate Directory's editor Becky Swann and nationally syndicated real estate columnist Brad Inman saw the possibilities early and have been keenly engaged in chronicling the Web's expanding real estate venue. Becky's IRED Web site, working in conjunction with Brad's Inman News Features, is widely recognized as a motivating force in bringing coherence to real estate resources and standards on the Web. Brad and Becky co-authored the following overview:

Ever get lost traveling down an unknown road without a map?

On the World Wide Web, homebuyers, sellers, investors and real estate professionals can turn to several maps to navigate the thousands of real estate sites on the Web. One of these is IRED News (International Real Estate Directory and News) at *http://www.ired.com.*

This site is a gateway to the technology marvel that is transforming real estate. Home loan originations, house listings online, electronic closings, and virtual walkthroughs are just the beginning of an electrified real estate market.

The IRED News site was created to offer the consumer and the real estate professional a comprehensive, independent, and reliable place to discover the vast resources on the World Wide Web. The philosophy behind the site is simple: consumers deserve to know more, and the real estate industry can be more straightforward, efficient, and helpful. The Web makes that happen.

IRED News is broken down into three basic pieces: the News, the Directory and How To. The foundation of IRED is the Directory, developed by computer and real estate expert Becky Swann, who realized in early 1995 that real estate is perfectly suited for the World Wide Web. Its interactive and database capabilities created a dynamic symmetry for the home buying and selling public to transact real estate.

Indeed, there has never been a medium better suited for showing the texture and details of a home and its interrelated rooms and spaces. Homes are three-dimensional, intimate, and personal, and the buying and selling of homes is tracked with statistics and sorted by lists.

All of these characteristics lend themselves to computers, with their graphic potential and their ability to churn and search through long lists of real estate market numbers and homes for sale in a given area. On the Web, for example, homebuyers will not only get a feel for the aesthetics of a house, but will be better informed as well about the value of their investment.

Becky quickly realized that the real estate industry would catch on to the value of the Web, yet would have no easy way of sorting through the thousands of real estate Web sites. The Directory and Becky's ratings offered a guide through that maze.

Growing like mushrooms

URL (Universal Resource Locator)
The combination of letters and numbers that uniquely identifies a Web resource.

"I gathered together all the URLs of real estate sites and began sorting them according to location. Forty-five sites were all I could find then," says Becky. "In November 1995, I had exceeded 2,000 real estate sites and in February 1996 surpassed 5,000. I suspect there are thousands more growing like mushrooms in the dark. I know there are a couple of hundred at any moment waiting in my email files for review and IRED listing."

Six months after the Directory was formed, Becky added news with editorial content from Inman News Features, the nation's leading consumer real estate information company. The news side of IRED (which can be found at *http://www.inman.com*) offers more than 3,000 pages of real estate editorial, including a vast library of consumer questions and answers.

Inman News Features also offers daily news stories on the real estate market, with the latest information on interest rates, tax law changes, industry developments, technology improvements, and real estate business stories.

The "Week in Review" lays out the week's top real estate stories in a news magazine format. Inman News offers consumers a help line where users can submit a question electronically and receive an editorial answer to their query. Hundreds of homebuyers and sellers use the help line each week.

The vast IRED News Directory is broken into U.S. and international real estate sites and is hotlinked to thousands of real estate Web sites. Becky does independent reviews of real estate Web sites; each month she ranks the top ten.

The reviews serve as a way to foster better Web pages. Keep in mind, most new visitors to a Web page will not give the time it takes for them to scroll down to the second screen, unless something they see captures their attention, excites their imaginations or fulfills a particular need for them. Visitors have other options, including the Stop button, the Back button, and the Home button. Of course, there is also the Off switch, or Solitaire, or Yahoo, or a Chat line somewhere. There are files to download, games to play, the Shopping Channel to watch.

IRED reviewers seek outstanding local information, unique approaches to the industry, clean and attractive design, useful tools and information, ease of use and navigation, appropriate, creative use of the medium and the technology without alienating less than state-of-the-art users, and last (and least) property listings.

Each month the ten top real estate Web sites are selected. These are the ten most creative, useful, and well-designed pages related to real estate sales or services as of the first of each month. There is no more specific criterion for the Top Ten. They are simply the best that reviewers have seen in the preceding 30 days.

Becky then ranks and rates hundreds of other sites with one of the following designations: hot, excellent, average, promises, obit, and don't bother.

IRED's rating system

Hot sites raise the bar on the quality of information or design on the Web for real estate-related sites. They may not meet all the highest criteria on all counts (ease of use, aesthetics, quality of information, and usefulness to others), but they meet most of them. Becky gives least weight to design, and most weight to local or other unique information.

A site rated excellent meets the minimum criteria for a pleasant and informative Web site. It uses the medium well, as opposed to simply presenting flat printed material in a Web setting. These sites are useful to anyone seeking information in a particular area.

FIGURE 1-3
IRED Real Estate Web Site for April 1996 (http://www.ired. com/dir/honors/ rehot.htm)

An average site is a typical home page. It offers information about the agent along with some property listings. It has little or no exceptional character. These sites are worth a look if someone happens to need an agent or is seeking property in that particular area.

The promises rating goes to sites that are probably new and actually do have promise for the future, but currently are not a good source for someone seriously looking for real estate information.

The next-to-worst rating is a résumé/obit. These sites are ready to be used as epitaphs. They feature a litany of offices held, organizations joined, photos of dog and kids, and a red Porsche with an agent surrounded by Sold signs. "Only a mother could love this kind of site. It isn't bad, just of no interest to a potential customer," says Becky.

Don't bother means the site is not worth the electricity to boot up the computer, and certainly not worth the time of a serious home shopper.

Of the thousands of real estate sites on the Web, says Becky, perhaps 10 percent have outstanding value and at least 10 percent more are useless.

IRED offers more than reviews. It shows the Web user the depth and breadth of real estate on the Web. There is information on foreclosure sites, vacation home Web pages, government agencies, trade associations, real estate libraries, new homes, commercial centers, and much, much more.

Of course, home listings are the emphasis of many real estate-oriented Web publishers. Some of the better ones include:

Seattle-based HomeScout *(http://homescout.com)*, which works with multiple real estate Web site databases (each with 100 to thousands of listings) to provide users with summary information on more than 200,000 homes nationwide. Once you view the summary information, a link will take you to the site where the full listing is located, often with photos.

Norwalk, Connecticut-based HomeWEB *(http://www.us-digital.com: 8080/homeweb/)* quickly recruited 300,000 listings, mostly among the national franchises, including Better Homes and Gardens.

California Association of Realtors' California Living Network *(http:// ca.living.net)* quickly claimed 200,000 listings from around the state. The site also includes consumer home-buying and -selling information.

Matchpoint *(http://www.nji.com/mp)*, a smaller operation from Milford, New Jersey, has sites in most states and Canadian provinces. Like Home-Scout, Matchpoint offers an automatic updating feature that emails buyers whenever a home meeting the on-file search requirements is added to the system or an existing listing changes.

For new homes, set your Web browser for CPS New Homes Navigator *(http://www.cpsusa.com)*, a Web site offering free links to 1,000 new-home developers around the nation. Visitors get general information about home developments and can then request more detailed data, including costs, floor plans, elevations, options, and the like via email.

Renters can surf to Rent Net *(http://www.inetbiz.com:1000/rentnet/ home.html)*. Rent Net offers nearly 300,000 units from 300 cities nationwide.

Beyond these listings, the Web offers a variety of services such as title, closing and mortgage information. IRED News helps point the public to various sites on home loans, including two sites where consumers can shop from hundreds of lenders for daily interest rates. They are *http://www.HFS.com* and *http://www.bankrate.com*.

For closing information, Data Track Systems (DTS) *(http://www. datatrack.com)* in Carlsbad, California, promises higher production and lower costs to the title insurance and mortgage industries and more efficient closings for the real estate agent.

In 1995, DTS created an electronic network solution that bridges the technology installed in title, escrow, and mortgage companies through a value-added Internet network. DTS uses Microsoft Back Office Tools, including Microsoft SQL Server and Windows NT. As a result, the solution is open to various technology platforms.

The high tech buzz phrase here is electronic data interchange (EDI). Throughout the data communications industry, real estate appraisers and lenders are among the first to move toward the new technology.

The Internet will soon make it possible for real estate appraisers and lenders to electronically transmit legal documents, as well as digital photos, parcel maps, floor plans, and signatures, across an office or across the country.

These innovations are transforming the appraisal industry and bringing greater efficiency to the typical real estate transaction. The changes are partly the result of technical progress, and partly caused by major lenders whose stated goal is to lower costs to the consumer.

While these developments are not yet widely discussed throughout the real estate community, most industry experts say that what the appraisers are doing today will eventually lead to changes in the way real estate is marketed, financed, insured, bought, and sold.

For brokers, sales agents, investors and homebuyers, a good place to start is United Systems at *http://www.unitedsystems.com.* Founded in 1982, this company staked its claim as one of the first to develop appraisal software. While the company specialty is high-end appraisal software, there are also electronic forms products for real estate agents, and all Fannie Mae and Freddie Mac forms in Windows format.

The home page for United Systems offers a menu of choices, including a free downloadable demo of appraisal software, an explanation of what EDI means to the real estate community, a discussion of photo imaging of properties, a list of appraisers using EDI, industry news, and a discussion of the potential of artificial intelligence in establishing the value of real estate.

The Internet is more than a technology tool for real estate. It will become a property assistant and house hunting detective for every homebuyer, seller and investor. It will become the new network for the real estate industry, replacing conferences and trade associations.

And for anyone in the property market, it will create presentation, value, and understanding like no other tool before it.

NO DOWNSIDE

So there's the upside of getting yourself and your office connected. What's the downside? Frankly, I can't think of one. But it should be pointed out that, all the hype aside, the Internet isn't a magic wand. It alone can't turn a money-losing office into a profitable one or make a bad agent into a top performer. What it *can* do is supercharge the office that is already doing well and wants to extend its reach and leverage its existing resources into more listings, more sales, and greater visibility. If that's you, then time's a-wasting. Let's get you connected.

Chapter 2 Connect to the Internet

The next two chapters are like the manual and the map book that will help you navigate this virtual universe called the Internet and get you where you want to go. Those readers who are more advanced may choose to skip these two chapters. If you decide not to read these chapters in detail right now, give them a quick read before we go out on the highway to explore real estate on the World Wide Web.

What does the Internet look like? How many ways are there to connect to the Internet? How do agents get the Internet into their offices to make it go to work for them? In this chapter, we answer these questions to help you better understand how to make this book work for you.

▶ What Is the Internet?

▶ How Do I Connect? Let Me Count the Ways

▶ What's a LAN, and Does Our Office Need One?

▶ Realty Connectivity

WHAT *IS* THE INTERNET?

To understand what the Internet is, think of a technology real estate agents are already familiar with: the phone system.

Plain Old Telephone Service (POTS) extends all over the world. When you pick up your phone and dial another phone, the phone company automatically routes your call through the available phone lines until the phone on the other end rings. As long as the phone you are calling is connected to the phone system, you can reach it. You can talk to anyone who is there to answer the phone.

Now, instead of a phone, imagine a computer at each end. That's basically the Internet. It's hundreds of thousands of computers, all over the world, connected in a way that lets other computer users call them up and access them. In most cases, the computers use the same phone lines the phone system uses, so connections get routed through available lines automatically. If your computer is connected to the Internet, you can reach any other computer currently connected to the Internet. You can view and retrieve any information on any computer that someone has made available to other computers.

In essence, then, the Internet is nothing more than a whole lot of computers communicating with each other. Each computer stores a variety of information and makes some or all of it available to other computers on the Net. If you have an Internet connection, you have access to every publicly accessible computer on the Net. If you choose to set up your computer as an Internet server, other computers also have access to whatever you make publicly available.

HOW DO I CONNECT?
LET ME COUNT THE WAYS

Making your initial connection to this collection of connected computers seems a daunting task. There are entire books devoted to Internet connectivity; what follows is a brief explanation of the primary ways folks connect to the Internet.

DIAL-UP CONNECTIONS

This refers to connections where you use your computer, a modem, and a phone line to dial another computer that connects you to the Net. There are several types of dial-up accounts.

Modem

A modem allows computers to communicate with each other over a phone line. At the time of this writing, modem speed or baud rate ranges from 2400 to 33,600 (33.6) bytes per second. The faster the modem, the more it will cost. Modem prices range from around $50 to over $400. At the time of this writing, 33.6 baud rate is the fastest modem available.

The faster the modem, the faster it will transmit data. Faster modems do cost more, but can save you money in the long run if you pay hourly for your connect time.

Multipurpose commercial provider

This category includes enterprises such as Prodigy, CompuServe, and America Online. These services all started out as closed systems; when you dialed in, you connected to their computers and stayed there. With the growth of interest in the Internet, all of these online services are providing access to the Internet.

You can think of these types of services as gated communities: someone has selected the materials for the system, keeping out materials they consider unsuitable or that won't attract a substantial audience. They contain a range of materials such as newspapers, Chat forums, stock prices, etc. You can choose to leave the gated community and enter the diverse world of the Internet. The commercial services also provide more guidance and often easier-to-use tools than many Internet Service Providers. Using one of these services is great for someone who has no previous online experience. If you are online a lot, these services can become expensive since you pay a monthly fee for a set number of hours for your account and then pay for each additional hour online.

The rest of the world—full-service Internet provider

There are companies that offer one-stop Internet access, known as Internet Service Providers (ISP). They provide all you need to connect to the Net, including an integrated software package that contains communication software, a browser, an email program, and other tools. The Global Network Navigator™ (GNN®) disk included with this book is an example of this type of account.

These services can vary widely. Some of them require you to use only their software. Others let you use your choice of software. (For example, you may have to use their email product, but can use Netscape instead of the browser they provide.) Since you can usually get a free month on one of these services, it may be worthwhile for you to try both and see which you prefer. Again, you generally pay by the hour after a set number of hours per month. This integrated service is usually as simple to set up as a commercial account.

Local or national Internet provider

This type of account is more for the do-it-yourselfer than either of the above. In this bare-bones scenario, the Internet Service Provider only provides connectivity. They usually provide instructions on how to set up your computer and how to obtain the software you need for your account. (Public domain software is free, but often lacks the advanced features and technical support of commercial products.) The

ISP may send you a disk containing the software or just tell you where to download it from the Net. They may provide a little or a lot of help in getting your system configured. You can, in many cases, upgrade to commercial versions of the software, but you do it yourself. Their service may be great, mediocre, or lousy. In other words, you have to do more homework to get one of these accounts up and running. Ask someone you know who uses the system before signing up, or ask the ISP for references.

So why would you bother with this type of provider? The main reason is cost. Most of these ISPs offer a service option that includes *unlimited* time online, for a very reasonable cost. A $20–50 one-time setup fee and $12–20/month is not uncommon. If you are comfortable solving your own computer problems, you may want to explore this option. This may all change now that the traditional long distance and local phone companies are jumping into the ISP business. Service may improve and prices drop as AT&T, Sprint, and MCI duke it out for your ISP business.

Within this category, you may have the choice of two types of dial-up accounts:

- A *shell account* gives you a text-only interface to the Net. You should get a shell account only if you are using an old machine and/or a very slow modem, and you plan to use the account primarily for email. Downloading files with a shell account is a tedious task. On the Web, you will not see any graphics or be able to hear sounds; you will only see text. A shell account is better than nothing, but at this stage of the Net's development, only barely.

- A *SLIP (Serial Line Internet Protocol) or PPP (Point-to-Point Protocol) account* is the most common type of dial-up Internet connection. Using a suite of communication protocols called TCP/IP (Transmission Control Protocol/Internet Protocol), dialing up with a SLIP or PPP account essentially makes your computer a "node" on the Net. You can use all the graphical Internet tools, and can upload and download files directly from the Net to your computer.

DIRECT CONNECTION

While a dial-up connection is great for a single user, when you start thinking about getting an entire real estate office online, you'll need to start researching your direct connection options. Direct (or dedicated) connection lets you connect multiple users to the Internet simultaneously. It uses digital rather than analog phone lines that have more *bandwidth*; this means the line allows more traffic to go over the wires than regular phone lines. Some common bandwidth terms you might hear are ISDN, T3, and T1. These refer to how much data can flow through the lines at one time.

A direct connection or dedicated line allows you to leave your computer or LAN connected to the Internet all the time. (Don't know what a LAN is? It stands for Local Area Network. See the next section, "What's a LAN, and Does Our Office Need One?") No need to dial into the service; you are continuously connected. This is an important option to consider if you want more than a few connections for your office.

Unlike a dial-up connection where the ISP maintains Internet service for you, such as Web hosting or mail routing, a direct connection requires that a technically savvy person maintain and troubleshoot the system at your office. Users' email accounts and Web pages can reside on servers at the office rather than at an ISP. While this situation gives you more control over your network and the ability to use the Net to its full potential, it does require more staff and resources, which are additional costs.

In the long run, if you are planning to have multiple users on the system, a direct connection can save you money by using fewer phone lines and modems. You also won't need to pay a service provider a monthly fee for each new account. However, the initial cost of

Bandwidth

The size of a network and its ability to carry data. The more bandwidth or larger the network, the more data can go through the network at once. If you have a lot of bandwidth, more agents can be online simultaneously.

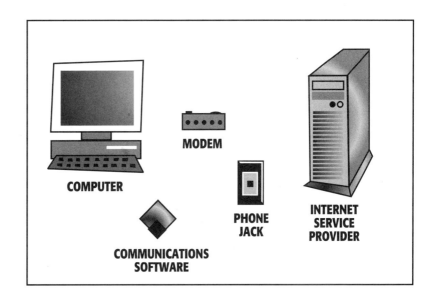

FIGURE 2-1

For a dial-up connection, all you need is a modem, a telephone jack, a computer, some software (see disk in the back of this book), and an Internet Service Provider or commercial service (also included with the disk)

Server

A computer whose main purpose in life is to provide service to other computers. For example, agents can access files on a server, putting them on their computer only when they need them. This system places fewer demands on individual computers.

installing the network and other equipment can be high, though increased competition has eroded the cost significantly in recent months, particularly for ISDN services.

Don't automatically be frightened away from a direct connection by the initial costs. In the chapters ahead, you'll see that a small office can do quite a lot with simple and cheap dial-up connection. But for larger offices and those with more ambitious plans, a direct connection allows more agents to use Internet resources simultaneously.

WHAT'S A LAN, AND DOES OUR OFFICE NEED ONE?

A local area network (LAN) is a network that connects computers and other peripheral equipment (such as printers) to each other in a small area, usually a building or a set of adjacent buildings. You can create a LAN by connecting all the computers in a room or in an entire building. This type of connection will make it easy to send files back and forth. A LAN usually has a server that allows users to share CD-ROM drives, printers, and other peripherals. By using a dedicated connection to connect the LAN to the Internet, agents in the office can access the Internet simultaneously without the brokerage purchasing many modems and installing several phone connections. Having a LAN and a dedicated line may have a higher initial cost, but is less expensive and more efficient than installing a separate phone line and modem for each computer.

A HYBRID SOLUTION: DIAL-UP GATEWAY (ALSO KNOWN AS NETWORK MODEM)

If you have a LAN, but don't have the funds to tackle a large scale direct connection, there is an emerging option called a dial-up gateway or network modem. Using a specialized piece of equipment that combines the functions of a modem and a router, you can use a single phone line to make contact with your ISP and have the dial-up connection provide Internet connectivity to all machines on your local area network.

Router

A piece of hardware that transfers data between two or more networks. A router acts like a postal clerk sorting mail into appropriate mailboxes.

This approach works best with small groups of five to seven machines, and can allow for various simultaneous sessions. Simultaneous World Wide Web sessions should be done with automatic loading of graphics turned off; otherwise, the system will slow to a crawl. Some of the newer boxes allow more than one phone line, thus doubling the effective speed of the connection. They also allow for upgrading to higher speed transmission methods, such as ISDN, frame relay, and fiber optic cable, when they become available. Check with your ISP, as they will ultimately be the ones who will have to make it work, and will therefore be most familiar with the equipment available and in use in your area. At the time of this writing, this type of modem costs around $1,000.

TIP When you start publishing on the Web, people, as you had hoped, begin visiting your site. The more people who access the site, the more bandwidth they will use, cutting down on the bandwidth available to the agents in your office. (In other words, your office network will slow down.) You can solve this problem by limiting access to your site or by putting your pages on a server outside your network, such as an ISP's server.

FIGURE 2-2

Different dial-up and direct connections affect the amount of data that can go through the lines at one time; this figure gives you an idea of how the type of connection you use affects your experience online

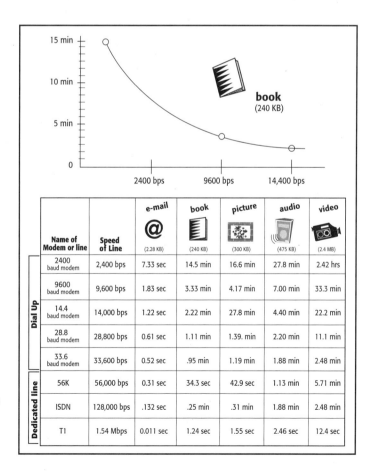

	Name of Modem or line	Speed of Line	e-mail (2.28 KB)	book (240 KB)	picture (300 KB)	audio (475 KB)	video (2.4 MB)
Dial Up	2400 baud modem	2,400 bps	7.33 sec	14.5 min	16.6 min	27.8 min	2.42 hrs
	9600 baud modem	9,600 bps	1.83 sec	3.33 min	4.17 min	7.00 min	33.3 min
	14.4 baud modem	14,000 bps	1.22 sec	2.22 min	27.8 min	4.40 min	22.2 min
	28.8 baud modem	28,800 bps	0.61 sec	1.11 min	1.39. min	2.20 min	11.1 min
	33.6 baud modem	33,600 bps	0.52 sec	.95 min	1.19 min	1.88 min	2.48 min
Dedicated line	56K	56,000 bps	0.31 sec	34.3 sec	42.9 sec	1.13 min	5.71 min
	ISDN	128,000 bps	.132 sec	.25 min	.31 min	1.88 min	2.48 min
	T1	1.54 Mbps	0.011 sec	1.24 min	1.55 sec	2.46 sec	12.4 sec

REALTY CONNECTIVITY

Most agents with computers at the office own them. Real estate offices seldom supply computers to their agents. And few have yet taken the big step of installing ISDN lines to speed electronic transmissions. But that's changing as more offices see the advantages of subscribing to videoconferencing services like Virtual Loan Officer on which they can originate mortgage loans for their buyers right in their own office.

Broker Chuck Scoble of Creative Property Services in Santa Rosa, California, recently did just that. His first Virtual Loan Officer unit, which cost more than $4,000 including the ISDN line, has so far been originating around ten mortgage loans a month. Chuck says CPS has considered networking all the computers in the office into a LAN so that they can share databases. But he can't identify ways that creating the LAN would enhance revenues to the brokerage, whereas the new videoconferencing equipment is already paying for itself. Chuck estimates that fewer than 10 percent of realty offices with computers have them networked into LANs.

Online Capital's John Hogan, who installed CPS's Virtual Loan Officer unit, says that even the most technologically advanced companies like Contempo in San Jose have LANs in fewer than a third of their offices.

Where the CPS arrangement differs from controlled business arrangements per se is in the fact that compensation for CPS's portion of the loan origination process goes to agents doing part of the application chores as well as to the brokerage. That gives agents specific incentive to use the in-house lender and to have a stake in the development of office technology.

Though CPS does not have a Web page, Chuck says he is attracted to the idea of getting his agents to use the Internet because they can create a low-cost office "intranet" at the same time if all the agents use an email service.

Like CPS, Online Capital is heavily invested in technology, but has yet to take to the Internet. Online has 24 Virtual Loan Officer videoconferencing terminals placed in various real estate offices and has 23 laptop-equipped loan officers out in the field linked together with Intel's Proshare. John says Online's growing relationship with the Homeseekers Internet listing service means that Online expects that its own business will benefit from the growing popularity of the Web as a real estate marketplace.

Larger companies like Contempo have a greater incentive to create LANs to coordinate communication and aid in broker supervision of agents. Contempo (Web address: *http://www.contempo.com*), one of the 25 biggest real estate companies in the nation, is also one of the most technologically advanced. Contempo president Robert Moles is more aware than most of the growing role technology will play in opening the real estate sales process to offer bundled services at the point of sale.

But even at larger offices, the volume of electronic transmissions today is seldom high enough to require even so much as an ISDN line—especially when laptop-equipped agents use the Internet itself as an inexpensive and multifaceted communication system.

Chapter 3
Basic Internet Training

To get the most out of your Internet connection, you have to develop some basic Net skills. As you spend more time online, you'll find a host of other resources and tools you can adopt. But for now, you should focus on the core skills required to get you on your way.

Earlier, we talked about email and the Web. In this chapter, we'll explain in some detail just how they work and how to use them effectively. We will also discuss two other key Net tools, the Web browser and the newsreader. For those who like interaction with their prospective Net-clients, we'll explain IRC, or Interactive Relay Chat. And finally, we will talk about actually constructing and publishing your own Web pages.

▶ Choosing Your Tools

▶ Nuts and Bolts of Email

▶ Joining Mailing Lists

▶ Newsgroups

▶ Interactive Communication Tools

▶ Using the World Wide Web

▶ Web Publishing

CHOOSING YOUR TOOLS

There are many sources for Internet tools: some are available for free online, others may come with an Internet account, or be purchased as a kit. For example, Eudora is a favorite email program, and Netscape is the most popular Web browser. You can download versions of these programs off the Net as well as purchase commercial versions (that come with end-user support) in software stores.

This book includes a CD-ROM that allows you to use the Global Network Navigator (GNN) service. GNN is an Internet access service that provides you with the software you need to connect to the Internet. Once you have obtained a GNN account through the software on the disk, you can download the GNN software tools for using the Internet. These tools include an email program, Web browser, newsreader, and Chat program. If you have a computer and a modem, you can install GNN and get started right away.

Here are some other ways you can connect to the Internet and get the tools you need:

A commercial online service such as America Online or CompuServe provides Internet access and an integrated set of tools for using email and browsing the Web.

A local Internet provider will provide instructions for you to connect to their service and download free versions of tools.

By chance, your office may have several computers with modems you can use for dial-up access, or it may have a direct connection. If a computer available to you is on the Net, you should have an email program and a Web browser on your system. If not, ask other experienced users at your office what programs they are using. More than likely you'll need to make a trip to the local computer store.

The important thing to remember is that users may have different sets of tools, just as they can use different ways to connect to the Internet and different types of computers. Yet these software programs all share a common set of basic functions. The purpose of the following tutorial is to introduce you to the basic functions of the tools.

AN OVERVIEW OF INTERNET SOFTWARE TOOLS

The Internet is a communications medium and the tools I describe here provide you with different ways to communicate online.

Dialer

This program, required only with dial-up Internet accounts, establishes a connection to an Internet service provider. Once you have the connection, your computer is on the Internet, and you can use the programs described in this section. The dialer is used to make the connection as well as terminate it when your Internet session is completed.

Email (electronic mail) program

An email program is a tool for sending and receiving email messages. When you get an Internet account, you get an email address that anyone online can use to send you mail. In order to send a message, you need to know the email address of the person you want to communicate with online. The messages you receive are stored on your computer or server. You can also join Internet *mailing lists* (often called listservs). A mailing list allows a set of people to exchange messages on a topic of common interest. When you send mail to the list, everyone who is subscribed to the list sees your mail.

The only real distinction between mail programs is whether you are using a graphical interface or a command-line version, roughly the same distinction between using a Windows and DOS program. A graphical user interface makes it much easier to understand the functions of the program.

The most popular mail program is Eudora. You can download the freeware Eudora Light for Windows or Mac (*http://www.qualcomm. com/quest/products.html*) or Pegasus Mail for Windows or DOS (*http://www.cuslm.ca/pegasus/*). Both are free, although QualComm also sells a more full-featured version of Eudora called Eudora Pro.

World Wide Web browser

The World Wide Web is a global network of information servers. Individuals or organizations publish documents on their own Web servers; anyone on the Internet can access these documents. Documents usually contain hypertext links to other documents or images. A Web browser is used to retrieve the pages from Web servers and display them on your computer screen. Most documents today include graphics and text, with an increasing amount of multimedia data as well (audio, animation, and video). In addition, a Web browser can get information from other types of servers, including FTP and Gopher.

The most popular browser is Netscape Navigator. Others are Microsoft's Internet Explorer and NCSA Mosaic. Netscape has begun integrating other tools into the Web browser so that you can use it for email and as a newsreader.

Newsreader

Usenet newsgroups provide yet another way for people on the Internet to communicate with each other by posting news on a distributed bulletin board system. "News" is a vast collection of daily postings on almost every subject imaginable. You can subscribe to various subject-specific newsgroups and read the news in each group using a newsreader. You can also use the newsreader to create your own postings.

Netscape Navigator now provides a newsreader, as does GNN, but most other newsreaders are public domain programs that use command line interfaces rather than a graphical interface.

Chat

Real time

Synchronous communication. For example, talking to someone on the phone is in real time whereas listening to a message someone left on your answering machine is not (asynchronous communication).

Chat, or Internet Relay Chat, allows a group of users to talk to each other, often at the same time. This method of direct, real-time exchanges does permit useful conversations, but it can be an annoying and confusing way to communicate. Nonetheless, it is very popular, especially with kids.

Chat is a text-oriented application, and users type in their remarks, which are shown to everyone in a chat room or channel. New, more graphical Chat programs are beginning to emerge.

Before the World Wide Web became a dominant application, there were several other programs that performed useful functions for Internet users.

FTP

FTP is an acronym for File Transfer Protocol. An FTP archive is a set of files made available on a server for other users on the Net to download. FTP is also a program used to send or retrieve files from an archive. You can now use a Web browser to get files from an FTP archive.

Server

A computer that runs software that allows it to offer a service to another computer.

Gopher

Gopher is an information server that organizes online information in easy-to-navigate hierarchical menus. Gopher is no longer widely used as a means of serving information nor are Gopher clients widely used now that the Web has overtaken their functions.

Telnet

Telnet is a program that allows you to log in to another computer on the Internet and have a terminal session.

The World Wide Web and email are the most widely used tools. Since you'll probably spend most of your online time exchanging email messages, and using the Web to access information and create your own Web pages, this tutorial concentrates on describing how to use these two tools.

NUTS AND BOLTS OF EMAIL

We talked earlier about using email as an essential Internet communication tool. In addition to simple text notes, you can also use email to send large documents, pictures, sounds, and programs as attachments. These non-text files can be attached to the body of the message in most email programs. When creating the message, you use the Attach function to select the file you wish to send. The user who receives the message must have the program required to read or view the file once it is detached from the email message.

TIP Check to make sure that the person receiving your attached message has compatible software to read what you send. Also, some commercial services don't allow you to attach files and send them to people outside of their service. You can still exchange messages with people using commercial service; you just may not be able to attach documents.

BASICS OF EMAIL ADDRESSING

Your email message needs an address for the person you're trying to reach, and a return address to show who sent it. A typical address consists of two parts separated by the @ symbol: the user's name and the domain where the user is known:

```
username@domain name
```

The domain name usually identifies the hostname of an organization, which could be a commercial business, a network provider, or an educational or government institution.

My address is:

skersnar@wco.com

skersnar is the username and *wco.com* is the host name of my Internet Service Provider, West Coast Online.

Most hostnames end in a three-letter identifier. These three letters indicate the domain of the organization they belong to:

- .edu   education
- .gov   government
- .mil   military
- .net   network resource
- .org   other non-profit organizations
- .com   commercial organizations

TIP An address must have all of its parts spelled correctly for it to reach the right person. An improperly addressed message will bounce back to you.

The users on your local network share the same domain, so you don't have to use the domain name with local email.

THAT EMAIL LOOK

The email arriving in your box looks very strange at first. There is a lot of verbiage at the top before you get to the meat of the message. These lines are called message headers, and most email programs give you the option of seeing the full header or just the important sender and subject information.

Bounce

A bounced message means that it is returned to your email address and does not reach the addressee. Bounced messages contain information about why the message did not reach its destination.

A barebones header looks like this:

```
From: becky@onramp.net

Date: Thu, 01 Feb 1996 17:33:37 cst

Subject: Re: Real Estate Agent's Guide to the Internet

To: scott kersnar <skersnar@shell.wco.com>

CC: Editor@songline.com
```

When you create a new message, you must supply the To field and, optionally, the Subject field and the CC (Carbon Copy) field. The mail program will automatically supply the From and Date fields when you send the message. There are often more than five fields in a message header, but those are the most useful ones.

A full header can be a truly impressive block of text because it includes all the routing sites the message hit before arriving. Since the

Net routes with no regard to distance, an email message sent from your neighbor across the street may get routed through three servers thousands of miles away, and each will be listed in the full header.

The header includes information about who the message is from, when it was sent, the subject of the message, to whom it was intended, and where the sender wants you to reply to the message. Sometimes you might send email from your home Internet account but want the recipient to reply to your office email account. So occasionally the sender address and reply address will be different.

After the header comes the body of the message:

```
Scott,

The more we can do by an interview the better. I am so
swamped that writing is a real bear. My computer is
running 18 hours a day just reviewing and updating
links, and responding to mail! I can talk and work,
though.

Becky
```

And finally, the user's designated signature file tags the message:

```
Becky Swann, Editor, IRED 817/481-4677

http://www.ired.com/

IRED International Real Estate Directory & News
```

JOINING MAILING LISTS

Mailing list

A conference/discussion group on a specific topic where all messages are sent to one email address and then redistributed to the email boxes of the list's subscribers. If the list is moderated, someone will review the messages before redistributing them.

When you go to an MLS breakfast you may be uncomfortable about standing up and pitching your listings like a carnival barker. And when the title company sponsors a free continuing education class on *Ten Fatal Property Defects That Lead to Lawsuits,* you may be vexed to discover that a conflicting appointment will keep you from getting some useful tips.

One way to practice pitching listings under safer conditions, and to stay tuned to the hazards of the trade that wise agents are talking about, is to join a real estate mailing list, or listserv.

Some such lists are overseen by an individual administrator who maintains an email address where everyone sends submissions— listings, buyer wants, questions, gripes, career decisions, etc.—and everyone else can respond to what they have to say. You can throw in your two bits on a subject or "lurk" in the background until you feel compelled to contribute. Sometimes you find inane discussions about whether Rush Limbaugh is an idiot or a genius, sometimes there are hot tips on mortgages, sometimes there are valuable discussions of key real estate issues. Generally, like all human interchange, these lists are a mixed bag. With some messages you'll read a few words and hit the DELETE key as you get the sense that the subject is of no interest. Others you'll save to read later, and some you'll read carefully and answer immediately.

The Net has spawned thousands of email-connected listservs and newsgroups on any subject imaginable. Most users agree that these groups will soon replace the old computer bulletin board (BBS) groups that became a mainstay of veteran online real estate practitioners. Monitored lists like the one Mario Giordani maintains at his Home Port Web site (*http://www.aros.net/~realty/realty.html*) tend to be ones that draw participants willing to stick to serious subjects; others have a variety of simultaneous discussions.

Whatever kind of group you decide to join, a word to the wise: learn how to unsubscribe at the same time you first follow the instructions for subscribing to the list. Since email distribution of these lists is automated, getting stuck on a list you decide you hate can develop into a real pain. Even if you like the water you get from a particular newsgroup tap, there are times when you want to turn it off (when you go on vacation, for instance). You are the one who has to remember how to do that. As one list administrator occasionally pleads in answer to incorrect requests to unsubscribe:

```
Folks,

Please [unsubscribe] the correct way.

send email to:

ListServ@property.com

In the body of the message write:

Unsubscribe commercial-realestate [Your Internet
Address]

Remember, you MUST use the same address/name to unsub
as you did to sub.
```

LURK FIRST, THEN JUMP IN

The netiquette for participating in Internet forums says you should stand quietly in the background to get the flow of things before expressing your views. If you come upon a technical interchange between veterans, it doesn't make sense to write back, "Hi, people, what are you talking about?" The following "want" message on behalf of a limited liability company is so obviously beyond the beginner's scope that few newcomers would be tempted to jump in and respond unless they had some idea what an LLC and UUcode were:

```
Reply-To: commercial-realestate@property.com
Resent-From: commercial-realestate@property.com
Sender: root@property.com
Subject: Bare Land
From: globeinv@reflash.com
Date: Fri, 12 Feb 1996 10:58:58 -0500
Organization: DEALMAKERS ON-LINE (609)587-4651

I have an LLC that wants to borrow $500,000 against
bare land it is purchasing for $1,975,000.

We expect to borrow on hard money terms: say, 5 points
& 15% rate. Time frame: 18 months, with no prepayment
penalty after one year.

The land as collateral: one parcel ($925,000) may be
encumbered with a first TD until paid. The other parcel
will need to subordinate to institutional lender to
build & sell single family.

If interested, let me know & I will email you an
executive summary. Best way is UUcode, using Word and
Excel files, so let me know if you have a fairly
current copy of Pegasus (which has UUcode built in) or
if you have UUcode.

Thanx

===================
Lorna Fastrac
GlobeInvest, Inc.
email: globeinv@reflash.com

===================
```

You may not be in this league, but you can't stay humble, shy and silent forever, so eventually you introduce yourself and tell the group what you have to offer. Remember, as agent Bill Hutchinson says, "No one can see you blush on the Net."

Your first submission to a particular list and its first response from an existing subscriber will look much like this:

```
>Hello, all!

>I want to introduce myself to the forum. My name is
Sam Smith. I am an exclusive buyer's agent. I enjoy
receiving the messages on this list and have learned
from them.

>Sam Smith

>Smith Realty

>11111 Strand Road

>North Fence, Nevada

>Sam@vcom.com


Welcome. My name is Freda. My office (as you probably
know) is in your part of the country. Check out the
listings on my Web site when you get a chance.

4sale4sale4sale4sale4sale4sale4sale4sale4sale4sale
           Freda Jones Phone: (000)555-1234
       Visit my WWW site: http://www.4s-s/~Freda /
    "We get it sold, no two ways about it, no excuses, no
                    fooling, no tricks"
soldsoldsoldsoldsoldsoldsoldsoldsoldsoldsoldsoldsold
```

ADDING PERSONALITY

That email signature is one way to make sure people get essential information about you in every email message you send. Some signatures are more lengthy, but a demarcated block of three lines or so is typical, something like:

```
**************************************************
    Will Your Exchange Fly with the IRS? Don't Worry,
                      Just Call
    John "Starker" O'Brien, your 1031 Advisor/Facilitator
         24 hr phone: 800-555-1234 email:
                johnobrien@xchange.com
**************************************************
```

You can raise or lower the aggressiveness of your signature's tone, but as you will discover, the signature block is a widely used email device to make sure people remember you and can respond to you without having to search around for numbers and addresses.

PERSONAL ACCOUNT

Larry Daniel
http://www.clad.net/
~realest8.html

realest8@worldnet.att.net

Netiquette
Polite and considerate
Internet communication;
following the generally
accepted guidelines for
Internet use.

Missouri agent and consultant Larry Daniel explains how to create such a signature:

The process of adding your email signature will vary a little depending on your software and whether you are using a server-based email program like Pine Mail or one of the programs residing on your own computer, where there will usually be a selection for Signature under one of the drop-downs on the File/Edit/Mailbox/etc. bar. This accesses a permanent file where you can type in your preferred signature.

Somewhere in the menu on a server-based system such as Pine Mail there will be the opportunity to access a similar type file where you can enter and save your signature. Just be sure to save it or it won't be there for the program to append to your email. One advantage to having your email program on your own computer is that several of the programs offer easy ways to turn off your signature when you want. If you have a particularly lengthy signature (which some consider poor netiquette) you may want to eliminate it when posting to a newsgroup or sending a reply to a message to someone you don't want to irritate or otherwise bother. Keep in mind that when you don't have it set to be appended you will need to attach some type of closing to the email.

TIP Many mail programs allow you to compose whole messages before coming on the Internet. You can save these messages and send when you are online. This feature can save you time and money by limiting the time you spend online.

NEWSGROUPS

Newsgroups (also referred to as Usenet news) also make it possible to send a message many people can read and respond to. With newsgroups, you use a newsreader program to read messages sent to the newsgroup. Newsgroups resemble large bulletin boards that address specific areas of interest.

You can read and respond to these messages on the Internet. When you reply to a newsgroup message, you have the option of replying to the entire newsgroup by selecting the Post Reply button, or you can send a private email to the person who posted the message.

Which to choose: a newsgroup or a mailing list?

Some people prefer newsgroups, some like mailing lists, and some use both for slightly different purposes. Here are a few tips to help you decide which might be best for you.

- If you don't like dealing with a lot of mail, use newsgroups.
- If you want to make sure others know you have posted a message, use mailing lists.
- If you want to see what others have had to say about a topic recently, use newsgroups.
- If you want more control over which messages you choose to read, use newsgroups.
- If you want to follow a discussion without having to go looking for relevant messages, use mailing lists.
- If you can't find a mailing list of interest, look for a newsgroup (and vice versa).

HOW CAN NEWSGROUPS HELP ME?

Many of the same reasons you would want to use mailing lists apply to why you would use newsgroups. Real estate agents use them for everything from pitching their listings to asking for advice on how to create a good real estate Web page.

To read and respond to newsgroup messages, you must have a newsreader. As with email programs and Web browsers, the type of Internet connection you have determines what kind of newsreader software you have access to. You may have a newsreader built into your Web browser; look for a toolbar or menu option that says News. If you don't have a built-in newsreader, there are several free or commercial products available. To find one, try Stroud's list for Windows applications (*http://cws.wilmington.net/news.html*) or the Macintosh Orchard (*http://www.spectra.net/~dsaur/usenet.html*).

TIP For information about real estate lists and which one might interest you, see Dave Moninger's real estate Web guide (*http://www.islandtime.com/re-intro/re-mail.htm*). To find more on lists and a guide to real estate newsgroups are, see land.net (*http://www.land.net/*).

FINDING NEWSGROUPS

It is generally easier to find newsgroups of interest than it is to find mailing lists. This is because newsgroups are organized according to a hierarchical structure, so most newsgroups that address a particular topic are grouped together in the list. For example, the *comp.* newsgroups discuss computer science and related topics; the *rec.* newsgroups discuss hobbies, recreational activities, and the arts; and the *alt.* newsgroups (probably the largest subset) discuss a truly mind-boggling variety of topics from Barney the Dinosaur (*alt.barney. dinosaur.die.die.die*) to censorship (*alt.censorship*) to Zen (*alt.zen*).

To see all the newsgroups available to you, you have to tell your newsreader program to show you this entire list. Look for a menu option such as Groups/Show All Groups, Options/Show All Newsgroups, or News/Get List of Active Newsgroups. The first time you request the entire list, it may take several minutes to download, so be patient. You can then scan through the list to find groups of interest.

Once the entire list is visible, you can scan it to find groups of interest. The list will not contain all the newsgroups available in the world; rather, you will see only the ones your Internet provider gives you access to. Your Internet provider determines which groups you can access, like a local cable company chooses which channels to carry. If your Internet provider does not carry a newsgroup you would like, ask your Internet provider to subscribe to it. (The organization that offers news to you may have policies about which newsgroups it is willing to host.)

Once you find a newsgroup of interest, tell your newsreader to add it to your active list of newsgroups. A menu option of Add Newsgroup or something similar should be available. If you later decide you don't want to continue reading the messages in this group, just remove it from your active list.

READING NEWS

Newsgroup messages are organized in *threads*. This means that a message and all its replies are linked together in a way that makes it easy to follow an entire discussion. Recent newsgroup messages are available online for anywhere from a few days to a few weeks, whereas mailing list messages are not stored anywhere online. This means you can find a newsgroup that might be of interest and immediately read recent messages posted to the group. This serves two important purposes: it tells you if the newsgroup is appropriate for your interests, and it shows whether the question you want to ask has recently been asked and answered.

TIP If you're looking for newsgroup messages on a particular topic, Deja News (*http://www.dejanews.com/forms/dnquery.html.*) lets you specify the text you want to search for, whether you are interested in recent or older messages, and so on. You can even limit your search to messages in specific groups or from a specific author.

GETTING THE FAQS

Almost all newsgroups have FAQs (Frequently Asked Questions) and their answers. If you have questions about the newsgroup, such as how it works and the topic it addresses, check the FAQs before posting a message. Many newsgroups routinely post their FAQs, while others just make them available for downloading. You'll find a copy of most FAQs for anonymous FTP download at *ftp://rtfm.mit.edu/pub/ usenet/news.answers/* or via Gopher at *gopher://gopher.well.sf.ca.us/ The Matrix/Usenet/.*

SOME WORDS OF CAUTION

When you hear all the hoopla about indecent material and pornography on the Net, the material in question is frequently found in newsgroups. In particular, there are a large number of *alt.sex* newsgroups that exist specifically to discuss and exchange photographs and text on adult topics. In addition, it's possible to run across foul language in almost any newsgroup.

INTERACTIVE COMMUNICATION TOOLS

You may have noticed that all the tools discussed so far allow people to communicate outside of "real time." That is, the communication isn't interactive in the way a phone call or discussion is. While this is usually fine, there may be times when you want to communicate directly with people who are online at the same time you are. The tools generally used for this purpose are discussed briefly in this section.

CHAT (INTERACTIVE RELAY CHAT OR IRC)

Internet Relay Chat (also known as IRC, or more generally, Chat) is a multiuser, multichannel chatting network. It allows people all over the world to talk to one another in real time. Each Chat user uses a nickname, and all communication with other users is either by nickname or by the channel that they or you are on. To use Chat, you either need to be using Internet access software with Chat capabilities built in (such as GNN), or you need a Chat program on your computer.

CU-SEEME

CU-SeeMe is a free videoconferencing program (under copyright of Cornell University and its collaborators) available to anyone with a Macintosh or Windows and a high-speed connection to the Internet. By using a reflector, multiple parties at locations anywhere in the world can participate in a CU-SeeMe conference, each from an individual desktop computer.

CU-SeeMe is intended to provide useful conferencing at minimal cost. To participate as a viewer requires only the free CU-SeeMe software and an audio-capable computer with a screen that can display 16 shades of gray. To generate your own video stream requires the same, plus a camera and digitizer.

There are people using CU-SeeMe all over the world. You can read about some of them in an online document called "In the Eye of the Reflector" (*http://cuseeme.cornell.edu/EyeofReflector.html*).

For more information and to download the CU-SeeMe software, go to *http://cu-seeme.cornell.edu/.* For information on enhanced, commercial versions of CU-SeeMe, go to *http://www.wpine.com/cuseeme.html*.

Internet telephones, which allow you to dial up directly from your computer keyboard, may well become a favorite tool for you (especially when prospects who have them are pleased to discover you among the select group of users). Check out Internet telephones at *http://www.Netspeak.com*.

FTP

File Transfer Protocol (FTP) allows you to transfer files from one computer to another. Computers that let anyone log in and retrieve files support what is called anonymous FTP. This means you don't have to have an account on that computer; you log in using the name "anonymous." Other proprietary sites require you to have a recognized username and password to access their FTP site.

Today, most people use the Web to access FTP automatically without even knowing it. For example, if you see a link that says something like, "Download the latest version of the software," the link probably goes to an FTP site. If you look at the address of the link, it will begin with the protocol *ftp://* instead of *http://*.

USING THE WORLD WIDE WEB

The Web consists of documents containing links to other documents. You navigate the Web by following links on a document, and moving backward or forward from one document to another. You can also browse directories that organize Web sites, much as a card catalog system does, and keep your own list of "bookmarks" you can use to go directly to favorite sites.

BASIC WEB TERMINOLOGY

Table 3-1 defines the most common Web terms.

TABLE 3-1 *Web terminology*

Browser	A user tool that displays Web documents and launches other applications
Home Page	The starting point for the set of pages available for a person, company, or organization; also, the first page your browser displays when you start it
HTML	HyperText Markup Language: the language in which World Wide Web documents are written
Hypertext	Documents that contain links to other documents; selecting a link automatically displays the second document
Image	A picture or graphic that appears on a Web page
Link	The text or graphic you click on to make a hypertext jump to another page
Search Directory	A Web site that indexes Web pages and allows you to search for terms you specify
Site	The location of a Web server
URL	The address that uniquely identifies a Web resource

LOCATING DOCUMENTS ON THE WEB

Perhaps the most astounding feature of the World Wide Web is that each document on the Web has a unique global address that allows it to be retrieved directly. This unique address is called a URL or Universal Resource Locator. Just as individuals have email addresses that locate a person within a specific domain, documents have addresses that locate them in a specific server domain.

A URL has three parts: the protocol identifier, the domain or hostname of the server, and the document's pathname. This follows the syntax for URLs:

```
protocol://domain name/pathname
```

On the World Wide Web, HTTP (or HyperText Transfer Protocol) is the *protocol* or language that browsers use to talk to servers. All URLs for Web sites begin with *http://*. Most Web browsers will communicate using other Internet server protocols, such as Gopher and FTP. Thus, you might see a URL that starts with *gopher://* or *ftp://*.

The next part of the URL is the *server* name. This might be as simple as the domain name, but usually it is preceded by *www*. This prefix is merely a naming convention that many follow, but it is not a requirement. For instance, either of the following URLs will take you to the default page for the GNN server:

```
http://gnn.com/
```

or

```
http://www.gnn.com/
```

However, if you try a site and find that using the simple domain name does not work, be sure to try prefixing *www* to it. If you have the pathname for a specific document, you can also supply it. Otherwise, you will begin at the default home page and you can navigate to the document using links.

It's often possible to guess at a URL. Almost every URL starts with *http://www*. Commercial site URLs generally end with *.com*, government sites end with *.gov*, and educational sites end with *.edu*. A company named XYZ Realty, for example, is likely to have a Web page at *http://www.xyzrealty.com*. Similarly, the URL for the White House (in case you want to express yourself on the home mortgage tax deduction) is *http://www.whitehouse.gov*.

A WINDOW ON THE WEB

A Web browser gives you a window to view the Web. Figure 3-1 shows a Web browser that starts at its own home page. This figure indicates the parts of the browser window. The menu bar allows you to access all the functions of the browser from pull-down menus. Under the File menu, you will find the Open URL or Open Location choice that you can use to enter a URL for a document you'd like to view. Next is the Toolbar, a set of graphic and text icons that provide easy access to most common functions, such as accessing your home page, moving back and forth from one document to another, and so on. One of the most important icons is the Stop button. This allows you to interrupt any document transfer, which is useful if you find that a document is taking too long to load.

Next, you will find the Location or URL field. It displays the URL of the current document. You can also use this field on most browsers to enter URLs directly. The URL that is displayed in this field may not always be exactly what you typed, as some Web servers translate a simple address into a more complex one.

On Netscape, there is a row of directory buttons, two of which are labeled NetSearch and NetDirectory. These buttons will take you directly to directories and search engines. I'll explain these tools in more detail later in this section.

The largest part of the browser's window is occupied by the document viewing area. This has a scrollbar which you use to view documents that are longer than what can display on the screen. Below the viewing area is a status bar. In this area, you will see messages about the document's status, including when it has finished downloading.

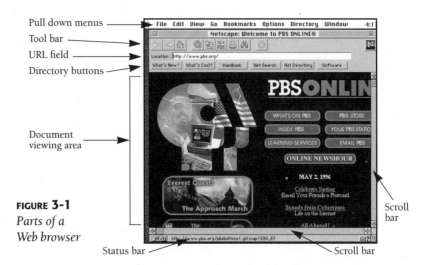

Pull down menus

Tool bar

URL field

Directory buttons

Document viewing area

FIGURE 3-1

Parts of a Web browser

Status bar

Scroll bar

Scroll bar

Also, if you move the cursor over a hypertext link, the URL will be displayed in the status bar, which is handy if you want to know where you'd be going if you click on the link.

Most browsers allow you to select which of these areas are displayed, so be sure to check the Options menu to see which areas are enabled or disabled.

TIP Remember that Web pages are constantly changing. Several months will have passed between the time these illustrations were produced and the time you read this book. In what might be called "Web time," several months usually means a myriad of changes and improvements to a Web site.

Let's navigate through a series of Web pages to investigate homes for sale in Evanston, Illinois, starting from the Web site, Internet Starting Points:

http://www.stanly.cc.nc.us/Links/Starting_Points.htm

Enter the above URL into your browser.

Once the document begins to arrive you can click on any visible link or use the scrollbar. You don't have to wait for the entire document to download. From the menu of search instruments offered, let's start by clicking Alta Vista with your mouse. In the space provided, type in *homes for sale, Evanston, Illinois.*

FIGURE 3-2

The Starting Points home page (http://www.stpt.com/)

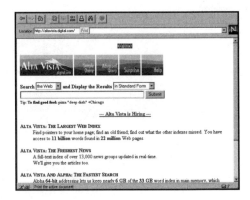

FIGURE 3-3

Alta Vista main page
(http://www.altavista.
digital.com/)

The first selection to appear when I tried that was:

```
Evanston, Lincolnwood & Skokie
```

```
Evanston, Lincolnwood & Skokie Property Listings.
Community Information. About Evanston About Skokie.
Community Listings. Attached — Condos and Townhouses.
```

```
0-150k /...
```

```
http://pruhomes.com/property/ev_prop.htm - size 848
bytes - 19 Feb 96
```

When I clicked on the hypertext, I moved to *http://pruhomes.com/property/ev_prop.htm*, the page shown in Figure 3-4, where I had the option of finding out more about the community of Evanston or looking at some Prudential listings.

As you can see, you can jump from page to page in a Web site, and, of course, a link may take you from one Web server to another in your search for information.

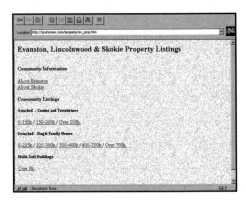

FIGURE 3-4

Prudential homes
(http://pruhomes.com/
property/ev_prop.htm)

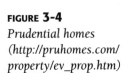

GOING TO A SPECIFIC PAGE

To get to a particular Web page, there are a variety of ways to enter a URL:

- Use a menu option or keyboard shortcut. Look for a menu option such as File/Open, File/Open Location, or File/Open URL. Often, there are keyboard shortcuts assigned to the options, such as CTRL-O or COMMAND-L.
- Type in the URL directly. Most browsers have an area that displays the URL of the page you are currently viewing. Type the URL of the page you want to go to and press ENTER or RETURN.

TIP A useful feature of Netscape is its ability to "build" a URL from partial information. For example, if you want to go to the URL *http://www.CompanyName.com*, you can type *CompanyName* as the location you want to go to. Netscape adds *http://www.* and the *.com* automatically.

Click on a toolbar button. Many browsers have toolbars that provide quick access to the most common browser tasks. Figure 3-5 shows a few examples of the buttons different browsers use that let you specify a URL to open.

IT'S NOT WORKING!

Sometimes when you type in a URL, you'll receive an error message indicating that the server is not available. If you check the URL for accuracy, wait a few seconds and try it again, it may work. Another solution for a particularly long URL is to delete part of the URL and go to the next directory. For example, say the URL you have is *http://pruhomes.com/property/ev_prop.htm*. If you receive an error message, try *http://pruhomes.com/property* or *http://pruhomes.com*. This will send you to the next directory up (or home page) where you can see

FIGURE 3-5
Toolbar buttons to go to a specified URL

the links available. The creators of the pages may have changed the page so that your particular link no longer works. Scrolling down on the home page *http://pruhomes.com*, you find a variety of options, including career opportunities with Prudential.

TIP An important point to remember is that URLs are case-sensitive past the domain name. For example, if you type *http://ERICIR. syr.edu/* or *http://ericir.syr.edu*, you will go to the same place. But if you type *http://ericir.syr.edu/COLLECTIONS.html* instead of *http://ericir.syr.edu/collections.html*, you will receive an error message that such a page doesn't exist.

DEALING WITH IMAGE FILES ON A DIAL-UP ACCOUNT

Not all sites have a special view of their pages without the graphics. If you are tired of waiting for images to download, you can do a couple of things to solve the problem:

- Turn off the images in your browser menu bar. While this solves your download problem, no images will reach you, just text. Sometimes the images are important.

- As the images are downloading, you can begin reading, using the scrollbar to the right to move you down the page.

- Hit stop! When you do, the images will stop downloading. This trick is especially helpful when you know the information you want resides on a different page: the link is there, but you're still waiting on the graphics. As soon as you hit stop, the page's graphics will stop loading and the rest of the text will appear. If you decide you need the graphics, you can always select reload, and the browser will request the page again from the Web site and retrieve it for your computer.

MOVING BACK AND FORTH BETWEEN PAGES

Once you've downloaded the pages to your hard drive (this means you've gone to the page by putting in the URL or selecting it through a hypertext link), you can navigate back and forth without waiting a long time. All browsers provide some way for you to move back and forth among the Web pages you viewed in your current session. As with opening a page, there are usually several ways to do this:

- Use a menu option or keyboard shortcut. Look for a menu option such as Navigate/Back and Navigate Forward or Go/Back and Go/Forward.

- Click on a toolbar button. Many browsers have buttons on their toolbars that look like arrows facing left and right. The left arrow steps you back through pages you have viewed and the right arrow steps you forward.

BOOKMARKS AND HOTLISTS

If you go to a page that you want to return to, your Web browser will let you add it to a list so you don't have to remember the URL or write it down. Some common names for these lists of saved URLs are hotlists, bookmarks, favorites, and card catalogs.

Different browsers store these URLs in different ways. Netscape puts them in a Bookmarks file that is itself an HTML document. The Internet Explorer for Windows 95 stores them in the same Favorites folder that you have access to when you use other Microsoft applications. GNN lets you create multiple lists, called Card Catalogs, that you can categorize by subject. For some products, you can even download or buy add-on programs that provide more management capabilities than the browser software itself.

No matter how your browser works, be forewarned that your URL list can easily grow so large as to be almost useless. Try to go through it from time to time and delete those URLs that once seemed important, but are now either defunct or no longer relevant to your interests.

FINDING INFORMATION ON THE WEB

What if you don't know the URL for a page you want to visit? Maybe you read about it somewhere and didn't keep the reference. Or perhaps you visited the page and want to return, but forgot to add it to your hotlist. Or maybe you are interested in a particular topic but don't even know if a related page exists. Search engines can help you find what you seek.

Search engines periodically scan the contents of the Web to rebuild their massive indexes of Web pages. Some search titles or headers of documents, others search the documents themselves, and still others search other indexes or directories. When you request specific keywords, the engines search the indexes they have built for those words. Your keyword search is not a live search of the Web, but a search of that engine's index.

Two features will probably influence your (and your prospects') choice of a favorite search engine. One is ease of use: it should allow you to customize searches without offering so many options that using it is confusing. It is important not to be overwhelmed by resources. Second, a good search engine should be accurate: if properly configured, it will return a reasonable quantity of fairly precise results.

DIRECTORIES

Directories are collections of resources that you can easily browse or search. Some, such as Yahoo, are large collections; others, like Internet Real Estate Directory (IRED), have a more targeted audience. People create and maintain these directories by combing other sites, organizing the information on their Web pages, and making sure the links to the other sites remain accurate. Some of these directories, like the Whole Internet Catalog, give brief descriptions or reviews of the sites before you go there.

Yahoo *http://www.yahoo.com*	Yahoo features a hierarchically organized subject tree of information resources. It offers limited search options, but is often a useful starting place because of its large database of authoritative sources.
Whole Internet Catalog *http://gnn.com/wic/*	The Whole Internet Catalog is a collection of Web pages organized by categories.
Internet Sleuth *http://www.intbc.com/ sleuth/*	The Internet Sleuth is less well known than the Whole Internet Catalog, but it offers a wide variety of specialized searches by category.

WEB ROBOTS

Web robots depend on software, rather than people, that automatically searches the World Wide Web for new material.

Webcrawler *http://webcrawler.com*	Webcrawler is lightning-fast and returns a weighty list of links. It analyzes the full text of documents, allowing the searcher to locate keywords which may have been buried deep within a document's text.
Lycos *http://lycos.cs.cmu.edu/*	Lycos is named after a quick and agile ground spider. It searches document titles, headings, links, and keywords, and returns the first 50 words of each page it indexes for your search. Its search engine is more configurable than Webcrawler.

Excite

http://www.excite.com

Excite currently contains searches of 1.5 million Web pages and two weeks of Usenet news articles and classified ads, as well as links to current news, weather, and more. It presents results with a detailed summary to provide you with an annotated selection.

To find the information you need, go to the search engine and enter terms relevant to your search into the form available. You'll receive a list of resources; each colored and underlined word indicates a link to that particular resource. Some pages will be more relevant than others, and most search engines list the pages in descending order of relevance. You can jump directly to each of the pages to determine immediately if they contain the information you need.

Not all search engines are created equal. That is, different engines find different pages, even when you give them the same search terms. This is because they differ in how they index and store the information in Web pages. If your first search doesn't turn up the information you're looking for, try another search engine. If none of them locates what you want, try using different search terms.

PUSHING THE ENVELOPE

Most of the hottest Internet development these days revolves around the Web. Audio, video, virtual reality, animation—it's almost impossible to keep up. Here are some locations for more information on some of the latest trends in Web development:

RealAudio™

http://www.realaudio.com

The RealAudio home page lets you listen to music, news, talk shows, and more while you are browsing the Web. If you have a 28.8 modem, you can download and use RealAudio2. If your modem is slower than that, use RealAudio1.

Java™

http://java.sun.com/

Java is a programming language that lets Web page developers add software applications, games, animation, and other features to their Web pages.

Shockwave™

http://www.macromedia.com/

Found on the Macromedia home page, Shockwave enables the playback of high-impact multimedia on the Web.

The VRML Repository

http://www.sdsc.edu/vrml/

Virtual Reality Modeling Language (VRML) is a developing standard for describing interactive three-dimensional scenes delivered across the Internet.

Web Review™

http://webreview.com

Songline Studios produces this online magazine covering Web technologies and the people who use and create them.

WEB PUBLISHING

In Chapter 7 we'll take up the question of whether you should build your own Web site or let someone else do it for you. Be assured of one thing: as you're about to see, anyone, from large corporations to young kids, can create and manage a Web site. It is this great equalizing capability of the Web that has fueled its incredible growth. The question you'll get a chance to think about as we move along is whether or not you can budget in the time to manage a Web site properly by yourself. If not, what you learn here will help you shop wisely for a service provider to do it for you.

Here's an introduction to the basics of Web publishing, along with pointers to sites where you can learn more right on the Web itself.

HTML—THE LANGUAGE OF THE WEB

When Web technology was first designed, the goal was to develop a way to describe the elements of a page's structure without specifying how the page should actually be displayed. In other words, the Web page specifies *what* to display, and different browsers decide *how* to display it. For this reason, the same Web page is available to anyone on the Net, whether they're using UNIX, DOS, Windows, Mac, OS/2, or any other operating system. If there is a browser that runs on that system, users of the system can view the page.

Every Web page is a plain text file that contains "tags" or codes. These tags tell the browser how to parse and display the file. The codes represent instructions written in HTML (HyperText Markup Language). You can use any text editor to create or modify HTML documents.

TIP You can learn how others code their Web pages. In Netscape, once you have a page up on your screen, select "View Source" from Netscape's View menu. That will show you a text version of the page, including all the HTML codes. This is a great way to learn how to get your page to look like one you admire.

HTML codes specify heading levels (as in an outline), paragraph styles, inclusion of images and sound, addresses of pages to link to, and anything else the browser needs to know. For example, Figure 3-6 shows how a browser displays a Web page (in this case, the home page for the Federal National Mortgage Association at *http://www.fanniemae.com*).

FIGURE **3-6**

*How a page may
look onscreen*

Figure 3-7 shows the text and HTML codes that make up this part of the page.

FIGURE **3-7**

*The HTML text of the FNMA page
(http://www.fanniemae.com)*

```
<HTML>
<HEAD>
<TITLE>Welcome to Fannie Mae</TITLE>
</HEAD>
<FRAMESET ROWS="70,*">
<FRAME SRC="/cgi-bin/header.ksh" NAME="Header" SCROLLING="no">
<FRAME SRC="/fr_main.html" NAME="Main">
<NOFRAMES>
<!— Include Java portion of standard header - TO BE PUT IN A FRAME —>
<BODY BGCOLOR="#FFFFF3">

<NOBR>
<FORM ACTION="/cgi-bin/navigator.ksh" METHOD="post">
<A HREF="/" TARGET="_top"><IMG SRC="/images/sm_fanniemae_logo.gif"
ALT="[Fannie Mae Logo]" ALIGN=middle BORDER="0"></A>
<A HREF="/WhatNew/" TARGET="Main"><IMG SRC="/images/icon_whatsnew.gif"
ALIGN="middle" BORDER="0" ALT="[What's New]"></A>
<A HREF="/General/search.html" TARGET="Main"><IMG
SRC="/images/icon_search.gif" ALIGN="middle" BORDER="0"
```

I won't go into detail explaining all the codes. Here are just a few this page uses:

- <HTML> specifies the beginning of the document.
- <IMG SRC> specifies a graphic (*welcome.gif*) to display, along with text that should be displayed if the browser can't display graphics.
- <p> specifies a new paragraph.
- <A HREF> specifies that the text from here to </A> is a hypertext link to the Web page in quotes. The Web page between the code can be a document you've created or a link to a URL on someone else's computer.

By learning only a few codes, you too can turn text into a Web page. A good way to learn HTML is to look at the source code of other pages you admire. You can select the feature to view source code on any browser. There are also a number of sites online that provide guidelines and instructions on using HTML. Just click on your Alta Vista bookmark, and type in **HTML primer**.

There are also a number of editing tools that make the process of writing HTML easier. These features include menu options or toolbar buttons for inserting the codes you want, dialog boxes to guide you through the options for each code, and the capability to check your pages to make sure they don't contain any errors.

Some of these tools are free. Most of the ones that require payment have demo versions available that you can download (copy to your hard disk) and try. If you like it, you buy it! Some of these tools are add-ons to word processors such as Microsoft Word, letting you author HTML from within the word processor. The following sites contain pointers to reviews and downloadable copies of a number of HTML editing tools.

MAKING YOUR PAGES AVAILABLE ON THE NET

Once you write your page, you have to put it on a Web server where the world can access it! How you do this depends entirely on the type of Internet connection you have. In brief, you store the page on an Internet server (usually on your Internet provider's computer) in a particular directory. The document can then be referenced by a URL.

The Stroud List
http://cws.wilmington.net/

One of the Internet's most popular and respected sites for reviews of, and links to, Windows 95 and Windows 3.x Internet programs of all kinds. Choose HTML Editors from the main menu.

**Bare Bones Software
BBEdit™**

*http://www.barebones.com/
bbedit.html*

One of the most popular text editors for HTML authors working on a Macintosh. Extensive HTML tools and extensions are available for BBEdit.

**YAHOO's Macintosh HTML
Editor List**

*http://www.yahoo.com/
Computers_and_Internet/
Internet/World_Wide_Web/
HTML_Editors/Macintosh/*

List of links to a variety of HTML editors for the Macintosh.

Publishing without learning HTML

Currently, HTML authoring is similar to the state of word processing about 15 years ago—you inserted codes into your document to indicate formatting styles and didn't know what the finished document would look like until you printed it out.

Today, just about every word processor prides itself on being WYSIWYG (What You See Is What You Get). A new generation of HTML editors is being developed that attempts to emulate a WYSIWYG environment for HTML authoring.

These "structured editing" products let you create Web pages without having to insert the HTML codes manually, and they will undoubtedly become more prevalent and sophisticated with time. They allow you to work with HTML as a set of structural elements rather than codes. You may find this easier to work with than standard HTML editors.

Here are pointers to a few of these editors. Most of them work only under particular operating systems. Check the home page to determine if a product will run in your environment:

GNNPress™

http://www.gnnhost.com/

One of the first WYSIWYG editors to be widely available, GNNPress provides a robust set of tools for authoring and managing Web sites. They also provide a server where you can temporarily store your pages for free while you are testing and developing them, as well as a permanent storage location if you need one. GNNPress is available at no cost to GNN subscribers.

Adobe" PageMill™

*http://www.adobe.com/
Apps/PageMill/*

Adobe PageMill Web page authoring software provides an integrated authoring tool and preview browser.

Netscape Navigator Gold™
http://www.netscape.com/

Netscape Navigator Gold integrates the features of Netscape Navigator 2.0 with Internet publishing capabilities, making it easy for you to see exactly how your page will look in Netscape while you are editing it. Netscape also provides storage locations for your pages.

Chapter 4 Learn from Agents Already on the Internet

Now that you have a grasp of Internet tools, we'll go see what some of your colleagues are doing with their real estate Web sites. To take an intelligent trip through the Net marketplace, you have to see it through customers' eyes. Computer software manufacturer Scott Cooley says people's interest in the Net boils down to "the three Es": education, entertainment, and email.

To have a productive Web page, he notes, an agent has to make good use of all three: offer useful information, keep visitors interested, and provide the means for the visitor to contact the agent through email. As we examine what some real estate Net veterans have done with their pages, keep these "three Es" in mind and ask yourself how real estate shoppers will respond to them.

- ▶ Like Walk-ins
- ▶ Up to Alaska
- ▶ New Hampshire Relocation Specialist
- ▶ A $900,000 Deal
- ▶ All Her Business from the Internet
- ▶ Her Web Site Doubled Her Business
- ▶ The Home Port Guy
- ▶ Learning as He Goes
- ▶ Hot Stuff

LIKE WALK-INS

Net-surfing shoppers act like walk-ins, only more so. Surfers have many ways to follow the whims of the moment. Prospects often walk in off the street clutching a list scribbled on an envelope or a fistful of marked-up real estate magazines, asking questions about a random array of lots and homes, price ranges, current mortgage interest rates, local job opportunities, and the most common local springtime allergies. In the same way, surfing shoppers are impelled by whatever they want to know and whatever happens to catch their eye. "Stop! Let's go look at that," they say to themselves—just the way they do from the back seat of your car when you're out showing property.

To offer you an idea of a typical surfer's mix of clear objectives and impulses, I jotted down some Web real estate pages on the back of an envelope. We'll take a careful look at those pages and deal with any navigation problems along the way.

First, a word of advice about net surfing. You are not a passive traveler on the Net the way you are when you click your TV remote control to change channels. You have to be careful to enter URLs (Universal Resource Locators, those strings of letters that begin *http://blah.blah*) correctly and watch your spelling and case when you enter them. Upper and lower case letters can make a big difference: get one wrong and your attempt to connect to the site may fail.

UP TO ALASKA

I went looking for Alaska broker Bill Hutchinson's Web page because somebody told me about his Kenai Peninsula photography and how he had turned hobby photography into a very effective real estate Net marketing tool.

I already had an email address for Bill—or "Hutch," as he's also known—but I didn't have his Web page address (URL), so I typed in "real estate for sale, Alaska" in the indicated box for my Netscape InfoSeek browser. Sure enough, one of the very first choices listed was:

Alaska real estate, Kenai Peninsula, Freedom Realty
  —http://www.corcom.com/hutch/realestate.html (Score: 54, Size: 7K)
  Alaska Real Estate. Welcome to the Kenai Peninsula where Alaskans go on vacation! And welcome to Bill Hutchinson's FREEDOM REALTY page. The Freedom Realty Team Photo. My name is Bill...(See also Similar Pages)

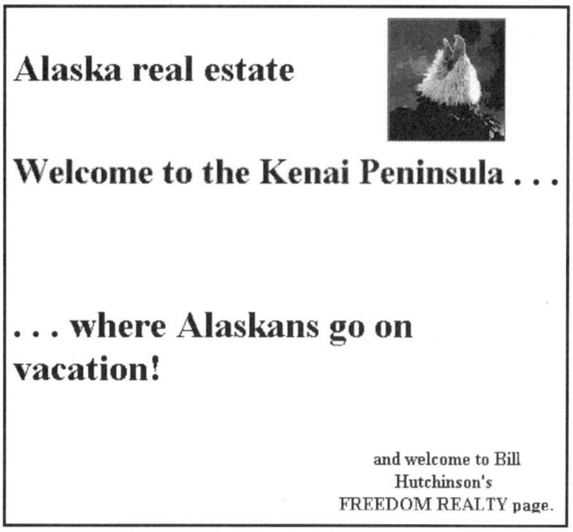

Alaska real estate

Welcome to the Kenai Peninsula . . .

. . . where Alaskans go on vacation!

and welcome to Bill
Hutchinson's
FREEDOM REALTY page.

FIGURE 4-1
Bill Hutchinson's home page (http://www. corcom.com/hutch/ realestate.html hutch@corcom.com)

I clicked on that with my mouse; in a few seconds up came a page with a simple eagle logo, welcoming me to Alaska's Kenai Peninsula, "where Alaskans go on vacation."

As I scrolled down Bill's page I found a number of hot buttons (hypertext phrases in blue letters) that, when clicked, brought up a photo of the Freedom Realty staff and led me to the information that Bill Hutchinson had been selling Kenai Peninsula real estate for ten years, when he wasn't traveling with his wife and daughter taking pictures of scenery and wildlife.

Other hotlinks took me to descriptions of Kenai, Soldotna, the Sterling Peninsula, and local shops and stores—some of which were listed for sale by Bill.

Then there were links that led to a few tidbits about Bill and his family followed by an announcement of his standing as "a Graduate of the Realtor Institute (GRI) and a Certified Residential Specialist (CRS)" licensed to work with both buyers and sellers.

The biographical links give a clear sense of just who this Bill Hutchinson fellow is. They personalize him and his company. Now, once comfortable with the host, the visitor is offered links to Bill's listings:

Outstanding three-story custom executive home adjoining fifty acres of Department of Natural Resources Kenai River Park.
Sit in your hot tub on the deck while watching the moose roam and eagles soar.
Five bedrooms, 3 1/2 baths, family room, mother-in-law apartment, attached 720 square foot garage.
MLS 28187 Listed at $239,000.

A return to the home page brought a notice that Bill can send interested people information about "hundreds more" homes listed by the Kenai Peninsula Multiple Listing Service.

Now, just in case the visitor wasn't already sold on moving to Alaska, the next link led to the home page for Kenai Eagle Press (owned by Bill) which offered a collection of stunning full-color photos of eagles, the northern lights and local scenery. Below the Eagle Press logo was a hot button for Bill's email address, followed by a list of links to other real estate sites around the country and links to government information sources.

Like most successful Web sites, Bill's includes a handful of links that have little to do with real estate. Building links to them for his visitor is a courtesy that makes his site more useful, a way of saying that the site has things to offer beyond listings and loan info.

Bill also made sure that, if his visitors are interested in buying a home, his site contains all the tools they need to make a decision. For example, one link led to a mortgage calculator, another to a do-it-yourself homebuilder information service

And finally, the most important link of all: at the bottom of his home page was a hotlink to Bill's email address. Clicking it triggers the browser's email function, allowing visitors to send Bill a question or salutation without leaving the site.

The resource-filled way the home page is laid out probably has something to do with long Alaska winters, the kind that encourage people to make sure they've stored up everything they need.

Working back and forth from Bill's home page to the other pages in his Web site—plus the other Web sites for which he provided links—could keep a buyer interested in moving to Alaska's Kenai Peninsula busy for a good hour or more. It would be hard for most people to resist taking one of the multiple opportunities to click the email button and send Bill a message with questions about eagles or winter temperatures or cabin building or motel prices or current mortgage interest rates or sights to see in Alaska.

A 1995 OLD-TIMER

Bill's Web site dates from May 1995 when he decided "to get a jump on the rest of the community" by putting up a page on the Internet. After surfing the Net to study other people's Web sites, Bill built his own pages by trial and error, using an HTML editor he found and downloaded from the Web.

Except for the money already invested in computer hardware and his Internet connection, Bill says he didn't spend a nickel on constructing his Web site—not for so much as an extra piece of soft-ware or a ten-minute consultation.

Within a few weeks, Bill's page brought him dozens of email inquiries from around the country. Based on these early responses, he began fine-tuning his Web pages. The first changes he made departed from merely creating a Web presence for himself toward "targeting viewers' interest in Alaska." He says he began to realize more and more that the same "Alaskan mystique" that drew him to the state was what was fascinating his visitors, and he decided to tune his Web pages to play on that strength. Creating links to interesting Alaskan sites became a major theme on Bill's pages.

To generate even more traffic he began sending his Web address to the numerous Net search engines and web crawlers in order to multiply the ways Web surfers could find his site.

This effort bore fruit quickly. Email from all over the world began coming Bill's way, from people simply saying they found his pages and enjoyed them, as well as from serious buyers who said they were ready to relocate to Alaska. Soon serendipity became his ally as news stories began to pop up about Bill's Web site and local advertisers hitched their wagons to his star, putting ads on his page to share his national notoriety.

Then the intended result actually happened—a buyer interested in a million-dollar property made inquiries. It was like deep-sea fishing and feeling that "big one" hit his line.

Though his exposure increased significantly, Bill's budget didn't. Until very recently, at least, he has been paying the same $25 per month to be on the Web that he paid from the beginning. "I do not spend money on links in the commercial sites," he says. "The whole Internet is too fractured for me to depend on the sites claiming to have the most influence. The usual search engine locations that allow free URL additions are sufficient."

Bill's biggest disappointment? "That multi-million-dollar buyer came out and looked at our market for a few days but decided to invest elsewhere." But Bill's hook is still baited. There are more big ones out there.

NEW HAMPSHIRE RELOCATION SPECIALIST

The Internet is already touted as the perfect marketing tool for the real estate relocation business. After all, when hard-charging laptop-toting executives get the word they're being transferred to Tulsa, where's the first place they're going to look for houses to buy? They'll turn to the Net.

So, working down my penciled shopping list of objectives for this surfing expedition, I set out to find Web sites that had something to do with the relocation business. Using the Alta Vista search engine again, I typed in, "New Hampshire and relocation specialists." Ten seconds later, a list of New Hampshire agents came up on my screen and RE/MAX broker Christy Day's name headed the list.

Entries for RE/MAX Relocation Services dominated the Alta Vista list of the first ten New Hampshire relocation specialists. The entries indicated that the search engine had found the pages under multiple relocation needs: travel routes, transportation, buyer's checklists, tax comparison charts, mortgages, as well as on entries for other real estate agents. In this particular search, by the way, only one entry came up unrelated to RE/MAX. Had that search been the sole evidence, you would have been forced to say RE/MAX had the relocation business all sewn up, at least for New Hampshire. These search results are the fruits of well-planned Web page construction. The search engine had keyed in on elements placed purposely on the RE/MAX page, in part, to yield just such a result.

When I clicked on Christy's page, the first thing that came up was a strip of red, white and blue RE/MAX logos across the top, followed by Christy's emerging black and white photo and her flashing 800 number.

Two quick thoughts here before we move on. First, Christy's choice of a black and white photo of herself was no accident. Though a color photo might have appealed to her vanity, she knew that color photos take longer to load on the user's screen.

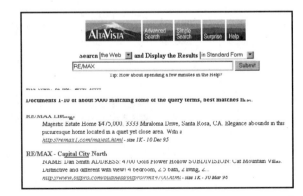

FIGURE 4-2

The Alta Vista Search Engine (http://altavista. digital.com/)

RE/MAX • RE/MAX • RE/MAX • RE/MAX • RE/MAX • RE/MAX

Christy Day

Real Estate Consultant
ReMax Country Properties
55 Ponemah Road
Amherst, New Hampshire 03031
Office: 603-673-9747
Toll Free Outside of NH: 1-800-222-2829
Fax: 603-673-8862

The RE/MAX Connection

When you choose Christy Day as your broker, you get an important bonus: a direct link to dynamic international network of real-estate specialists. ReMax gives you the visibility of national media advertising and the quality of a professionally managed local agency

FIGURE 4-3
*Christy Day
(http://www.
nhrelocation.com/
christy.html)*

About that flashing 800 phone number. When the 800 number is the sole way offered to reply immediately, you do want to encourage visitors to use it, though many Net aficionados look askance at flashing elements on a Web page. On the other hand, a flashing "SOLD" over a listing projects an image of success and movement. With the increasing availability of moving elements for Web pages, you will face choices like these when creating your own page.

What came next on Christy's page was a statement about the RE/MAX Connection:

When you choose Christy Day as your broker, you get an important bonus: a direct link to a dynamic international network of real-estate specialists. RE/MAX gives you the visibility of national media advertising and the quality of a professionally managed local agency.

After introducing RE/MAX, Christy used the next link to introduce herself, including an impressive list of her professional awards, offices and sales accomplishments. There followed a few highlights from her personal history (grew up on a Wyoming ranch, graduated cum laude from Radcliffe, lives in Amherst with her two daughters, has a wide variety of interests and hobbies). There was a bold invitation to "CALL Christy today for all your tough real estate issues!" But there was no email link to Christy. There was an email link to RE/MAX, but none to Christy.

I called the flashing 800 number, got a live person and left a message with Christy's voicemail to call me back. (When she returned my call, Christy said she planned to add a personal email link soon.)

The message that she has been in the "top 10 percent in gross sales since 1983" lets us know that Christy is a genuine top producer, but the impression I got from the omission of an email link was that Christy didn't (yet) rely on her Web site to generate much business.

However—as you well know—she's still far ahead of most agents in developing a presence on the Web.

Christy told me she still spends $300–500 a month on advertising, most of it in magazines. But, she added, now that she has received around ten legitimate inquiries and one genuine relocation buyer in her first several months on the Net, she intends to invest more time and money on her Web site to increase its interactivity, sophistication, and number of pages.

After I left my message for Christy I went on to surf the RE/MAX circuit by clicking the mouse to "View RE/MAX listings on the Home-WEB." Guess what? The relocation specialists had relocated:

RE/MAX International on the Internet

Has MOVED!

Our new address is:

http://www.remax.com

The message, though a bit frustrating, was better than the alternative, a faceless error message saying the page no longer resides at that site. From time to time you may decide it's in your interest to move your Web site, generally because a different Internet service provider offers a lower price. When you move to that provider, your site address will change as well. If this happens, always leave a forwarding address for a time at your old service provider. Some will do this for 30 days as a free service. Others will require that you continue to pay for as long as you want the referral page up. Some consider 90 days the minimum time a referral page should stay active. Even if you are charged $25 a month for an Internet account you no longer need, it's well worth it. Six months would be optimum.

FIGURE 4-4
*RE/MAX
(http://www.remax.
com/
email: webmaster@
remax.com)*

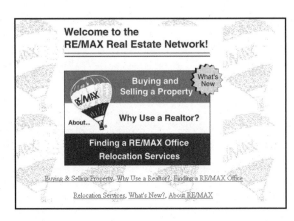

Also, the new URL listed in the "We've Moved" referral page should always be a hotlink. You've already inconvenienced your customer a bit by moving, so don't make them type in your new URL as well. (One important message was missing from the RE/MAX referral notice. Always remind your users to "remember to update your bookmarks" so that surfers don't keep coming back to the referral page if they have the old address saved.)

Once I connected to the main RE/MAX page, I was disappointed. I hit the link and waited and waited and waited as another picture of the RE/MAX balloon logo drew slowly on my screen. Then came…another RE/MAX balloon. It was like a slow motion scan of a stack of inserts in the Sunday newspaper: all logos and hype, no houses for sale. The redundant images definitely were not worth waiting for.

Obviously, the RE/MAX main office had decided it was time to stake out a claim on the Web, but saw it at that point as some kind of cyber-extension of its real estate magazine ads. But that was then. We'll find Christy and RE/MAX in the thick of things as the Web marketplace evolves.

A $900,000 DEAL

Some people know *exactly* what they want to do with their Web pages. While they may not use every Java trick, Netscape upgrade and hot plug-in as soon as it arrives, they never linger behind for very long.

To find an example, let's take a look at a prize-winning real estate Web site. If you made a bookmark for Bill Hutchinson's home page, you can go back to it to use Bill's link to the Internet Real Estate Directory and find the list of IRED's "Top Ten Real Estate Sites" for the month. For this particular search, I scrolled down until I found a commercial site, Seattle CCIM Gregory Laycock's Grubb & Ellis page.

One thing you can't help noticing about Greg's page is that (like the IRED home page before it) it comes up quickly because there are no developing photos at the top of the page to impede progress. As you scroll down (past the list of hyperlinks to other pages in this site) you find an email button at the bottom of the page. Remember those three factors and how they relate back to Scott Cooley's three Es: no boring wait, a bunch of hyperlinks to promising-looking information, and an email opportunity to interact with the host of the page.

When you scroll back up Greg's page to the hyperlinks, you gain access to a wealth of detailed information about the Seattle area Greg serves. These links can be invaluable to an out-of-town investor trying to get a feel for the area. Greg's hypertext site links are:

Seattle Industrial Land Report
Puget Sound Apartment Report
The Valley Watch Industrial Newsletter
King County Investment Review
The Office Viewpoint
Hospitality News Report
Puget Sound Retail Report
Eastside Commercial Sales Report
Market Flash
Tech Trends

Reports on all these areas tend to begin with summaries of average cap rates and samples of market activity, and then go into the nitty-gritty. The depth of analysis offered, given the Web's prevailing quick-hit nothing-detailed standard, is remarkable.

Following those pages are hyperlinks to Greg's current listings for Seattle, categorized as Apartment, Retail, Industrial, Land, Office, Hospitality, or Special Purpose.

Then come current market trends and forecasts for the Puget Sound/Seattle area followed by hyperlinks to "Other Interesting Web Sites," including IRED, professional organizations and Net search

FIGURE 4-5
Grubb & Ellis (http://www.realtynet. com/ USA/WA/Seattle/gali/ Gali.html 74631.2131@ compuserve.com)

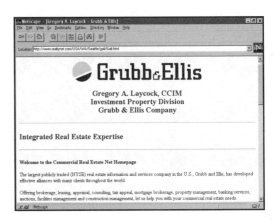

engines. Greg emphasizes that the most important features of good pages are that they come up quickly and have a good mix of attractions and features to hold visitor interest.

Greg designed his page and made his own hyperlink decisions, but he hired Nichole Engel of Internet Solutions in Seattle to do the actual HTML programming. "Hire an expert and spend your time on your own business" is Greg's advice. "Don't let technology drive your business, let the business drive the technology." He says he constantly adds directories and more content to his site—which, he estimates, costs him $350 per month to maintain.

"The biggest obstacle I encountered," he says, "was the resistance of the company I work with allowing me to go on the Internet with market research information. They feared providing too much information to our competitors. Once my Web page was established, the local media and newspapers featured an article about the World Wide Web and discussed interesting Web pages, naming my home page as one of them."

So far, Greg says, he can credit at least one completed $900,000 deal to his Web site. Less than 30 days after the page went up, Greg received an email inquiry from a prospect who wanted a complete proforma, spreadsheets, pictures and so on emailed back right away so that he could take a careful look and play with the numbers. More email questions followed the next day, followed by notice that the buyer would make an offer. The offer arrived by email (with scanned-in signature).

Everything during that first 48 hours was done by email—no phone calls, no faxes, no snail mail. Then, once the contingent contract was signed and the due diligence process began in earnest, things slowed down. Three or four months later, the deal closed. Greg didn't say what his commission was on the deal, but even if it was just 3 percent, that's $27,000. You calculate for yourself how long, at $350 a month, that one sale will pay for Greg's Web site.

Greg says that so far the biggest Web benefits he's seen have been marketing himself and professional networking. "I've wound up having a couple of additional clients from outside the U.S.—Canada and Hong Kong—and some from California, including an institutional pension-fund advisor."

"The benefit that I see from my Web site is not necessarily putting up listings," he says, "it's market info about the area and myself. When someone calls me up and asks what's happening, I can say, 'Check it out on my Web site.'"

ALL HER BUSINESS FROM THE INTERNET

The next site I visited was one I saved from the following posting on a real estate list:

> I've had my email address on my card for 6 months, my URL on my card for four months. All, repeat, ALL my business comes from the Internet. I went online in August [1995]. It was just in the last three weeks that I persuaded a loan officer to get a computer and email. He's already gotten business from it. I told my broker 9 months ago that I was going to go on the Internet and he said "What is the Internet?" He knows now. I would love to save those long distance charges with more email users.

All her business from the Internet? I definitely wanted to hear more about that, so I copied the URL provided in the signature block at the bottom of Lenn's message, closed Eudora, opened Netscape, and pasted the address in.

If you find yourself getting impatient waiting for Lenn Harley's Homefinders page to come up on the screen, you really need to upgrade your modem, because Homefinders is designed to jump up like a trained seal going after a piece of fish. Starkly simple graphics, no picture, and no wait. You can traverse the page from top to bottom in a flash. You get the message in one dose:

HOMEFINDERS

A Homebuyer's Real Estate and Relocation Service

WHO WE ARE: A real estate homebuyer's service for Maryland and Virginia.

FIGURE 4-6

Homefinders home page (http://www. homefinders.com lenh@homefinders.com)

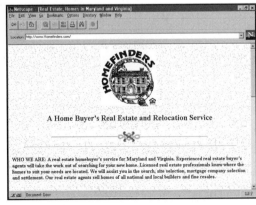

Experienced real estate buyer's agents will take the work out of searching for your new home. Licensed real estate professionals know where the homes to suit your needs are located. We will assist you in the search, site selection, mortgage company selection and settlement. Our real estate agents sell homes of all national and local builders and fine resales.

Then come your choices in hypertext invitations to visit other pages:

More about Homefinders' Real Estate Services
Click here to begin your home buying adventure!

How Much Home Can I Buy?
Click here to determine your price range and best financing options.

Where Do I Want To Live?
Take a tour with us to many attractive homes in Maryland and Virginia.

Hampton Roads
Click here for Hampton Roads area map, sample houses and tax rate information.

Please Have an Agent Contact Me.
Click here to send your home search needs to one of our Homefinders buyer agents.

Frequently Asked Questions (FAQ)
Click here to get answers!

Then comes an invitation to other agents to offer their services on the Homefinders site, and a mortgage primer and loan calculator for buyers.

The homeviewing option brings up Maryland and Virginia areas on a map, then photos of individual listings in categories (condos, single family dwellings, etc.) indicating average price range for comparable offerings. Selecting Hampton Roads brings the following message, followed by more photos and another opportunity to hit the loan calculator:

HOMEFINDERS is a real estate homebuyer's service for areas of Virginia and Maryland. South Hampton Roads cities served include Virginia Beach, Norfolk, Chesapeake, Portsmouth and Suffolk. Our experienced real estate buyer's agents will take the work out of searching for your new home. Our professionals are relocation experts, and will begin helping you immediately, and will stay with you every step of the way! They will assist you in finding that dream home, selecting a suitable financing alternative, setting up a professional home inspection, and seeing you through to a successful settlement.

At the bottom of each of Lenn's pages is a hypertext email invitation. The whole package is clean and reassuringly simple.

Lenn says she started getting results about 30 days after she first built her Web page in 1995 to reach out to relocation buyers. She stuck with it because it was productive and fun, especially receiving email from Germany and Japan and messages complimenting her on her site.

Lenn helped design her site; she uses her Internet Service Provider (ISP)—Cyber Services Inc. of Vienna, Virginia (*http://www.cs.com*)—to code and maintain her pages.

"It took about a month to design and build and cost $1,500. We are changing constantly whenever I think it will improve the content, when rates change, and when I add another agent in another market area." She says adding a hyperlink to a loan officer she deals with regularly was one of the most important changes she's made.

The expense so far has been more than offset by the money she's saved on other forms of advertising, Lenn says, because now her Web presence is her *only* advertising.

While I was looking at Lenn's Homefinder page, I received email from her:

```
X-Sender: lenh@cyber.cs.com
Date: Sat, 27 Jan 1996 18:42:11 -0500
To: scott kersnar <skersnar@shell.wco.com>
From: Lenn Harley <lenh@homefinders.com>
Subject: Re: (no subject)
```

Hi Scott: I am receiving sufficient direct inquiries from buyers from the Internet to keep me busy, either showing property, previewing, touring, researching or, thank goodness, closing sales. I have referral business, but all my NEW business from advertising is from the Net. It is the only advertising I do.

I have met three local buyers through the Internet; everyone else has come from out of town, Japan, Germany, Texas, South Carolina, Spain, California, etc.

The main downside I see here is that it takes some time for out of town buyers to actually get here. I can't sell them till they are here.

As more and more agents join the Net, the number of respondents may diminish. Or perhaps this will be overcome by the additional number of folks on the Net.

```
We'll see. I guess by then I'll have to incorporate
Java scripts to get their attention.
```

HER WEB SITE DOUBLED
HER BUSINESS

If you search "real estate offices, Scottsdale, Arizona" with the Yahoo or Alta Vista search engine, one of the first names that comes up is Alice Held. Though Coldwell Banker agent Alice Held has been picked as a Web "Cyber Star," by Allen F. Hainge Seminars and written up in the *International Herald Tribune*, she is not at all vain about her Web site. When I first spoke with her on the phone, in fact, she ticked off two flaws she was anxious to correct on her Web page. The first was that she needed to add a hotel page because an out-of-town customer has just been misled by information linked to her site into staying in a disappointing hotel. She sounded as though she had inadvertently sent her best friends to spend the night in a flophouse.

The second thing she said, when I told her that her home page was a favorite of mine, was that she was going to reduce the photograph at the top of her home page because IRED editor Becky Swann told her the photo made her page come up too slowly.

Though she is perfectly willing to talk about flaws and needed improvements, Alice stresses that she would never besmirch a Web page with "Under Construction" notices; nothing will ever go up on her page unfinished. Her brother suggested and built the page for her, but Alice, a CRS recognized for her innovative relocation program, oversees it meticulously. Alice might remind us that a well-bred page does not perspire, nor does it bore its guests with apologies.

FIGURE 4-7

Alice Held – Coldwell Banker Success Realty home page (http://www. primenet. com/~alheld/ come2az@primenet. com)

As you scroll down Alice's page you find it dotted with invitations to contact her by email or at her toll-free number. You learn that she has sold real estate for more than 20 years in New York, Hawaii (where she retains a license), and Arizona, where she returned after finding that she didn't like a tropical climate.

If you're thinking of buying a home in Scottsdale, a free Newcomer's Package is yours for the asking when you fill out a buyer's profile with your email and street address. This is an important Netmarketing tool: give your visitors something of value before you ask for something in return. As you well know, having visitors fill out a prospect form—especially one that goes right into your database—gives you all the contact information you need to follow up later.

Alice's page also serves up some listings to look at right off the bat, in an order that can't help engaging your curiosity and leaving an impression of Alice herself as a cosmopolitan and intriguing agent. Of the three "luxurious homes" presented, the first was a $499,000 penthouse on the island of Phuket in Thailand; the second a Diamond Head penthouse in Hawaii, and the third a Scottsdale "Oasis of Endless Tranquillity." What a way to frame Scottsdale as a world class area!

Alice then offers a hot button list of local amenities: information on Arizona sunshine, tennis, the arts, master planned communities, employers, schools, nearby communities, and weather—plus an affordability calculator.

On the page for ordering her Newcomer's Package, Alice gracefully encourages inquirers to prequalify themselves "so that we can include some listings in your price range." Here she places a link to a mortgage prequalification calculator so visitors can get a feel for the their comfortable price range. She also includes an invitation to subscribe to her printed newsletter. Everything on the page builds an atmosphere of connection and interaction.

Though her brother constructed the page, Alice says she "hired someone who solicited my business by contacting me, to register me with all the major search engines and real estate sites." There are people who will charge you to do this, but the procedure is simple and you can easily do it yourself in your spare time. Each search engine's home page includes a link to the registration page where you sign up.

Alice says her Web site has doubled her business, with many of her buyers coming from other countries, principally Canada, but also Sweden, Germany and South Africa.

Because she deals with so many customers from other countries, one of the additions Alice will make the next time she remodels her Web site is to add a page on immigration problems and laws.

THE HOME PORT GUY

The email I received from Lenn Harley came to me by way of a forum on the Home Port, the Web site of Wardley Better Homes and Gardens top producer Mario Giordani. Weeks after I contacted Mario about this book, I received an email message about his site:

> The Home Port, one of the first pioneers on the Internet, is now going through a face-lift. The site is designed for fast computers with a minimum of 256 colors and a 28.8K connection. We invite all to take a look at our newly remodeled Web site—which still has a few more things to be added and changed within the next few weeks.

I punched up his page and waited for the usual full-length black-and-white photo to pop up showing Mario talking on his cellular phone. Instead up came 3-D letters blocked out like monolithic slabs of granite: THE HOME PORT.

This is not the first time Mario has changed his page. When he makes a change, he uses the discussion group he monitors from his site as a focus group to get feedback. This time he encountered some resistance. Some people subscribing to his group questioned Mario's talk about high-tech color resolution and ultrafast modems aimed at attracting impatient well-heeled Net surfers.

Though the decorative quality of Mario's site keeps improving, he says the main changes he makes are to increase user friendliness. "I have added background music and sounds, but you have to be running Windows 95 and the Microsoft Internet Explorer 2.0 to hear it."

Mario believes "you have to make your page very attractive and eye-catching, whether you care about things like that or not. If you can't do it, hire someone else to do it. Mediocre-looking pages don't get results."

FIGURE 4-8

Home Port from Mario Giordani Wardley Better Homes & Gardens Realty (Realty@aros.net)

With a background in software marketing and experience running a BBS, Mario had been one of the early real estate agents to have a significant presence on the Internet. His site has been featured in *Real Estate Today* magazine as one of the pioneering best sites on the Web.

Mario's initial cost to build his site (given his technical background) was only $300. After that the biggest investment was time. He credits his Web site for putting him at the top of the heap of 1,500 Wardley Better Homes and Gardens agents throughout the state of Utah.

Though Mario tracks the number of hits his site gets every week, he says the measure he really values is the business his site draws. In particular, he watches how many homes he actually sells *local* buyers who were attracted by his Web pages. Despite the national exposure his Home Port forum has brought him, successfully promoting himself in his local market is the reward he mentions again and again. Mario says it took six months to a year before he started to see the kind of results he gets now: "Most people are just browsing, not buying."

Mario offers one of the more active Net discussion forums that are coming to supplant older BBS groups. When you hit the button on Mario's page for the discussion group, what comes up first is an announcement:

Express yourself! Join a list today!

An explanation follows that this real estate mailing list "has been designed for the discussion of real estate related topics, announcements of new real estate sites, exchange of information, techniques, sales and marketing of real estate, exchange of referrals and real estate-related software topics." Then comes a Major-Domo email form for you to fill out if you want to subscribe to the list—all very easy, all very convenient.

Above the "join list" button is the hypertext message "unsubscribe from list." As I noted earlier, it's always a good idea to find out how to get off a list once you've subscribed, and Mario puts this information right at the visitor's fingertips. Clicking the "join list" button adds your name to the list of Home Port subscribers. Here real estate professionals can put themselves in the flow of real estate opportunity, leads, contacts, arguments and information on a host of topics that can keep you in the know and out of hot water. A quick read through Home Port or Dealmakers messages every day is easily equivalent to attending a couple of continuing education classes a year.

These lists also provide a good place to pitch your listings. Mario recently has added a free residential listing service to his list:

Date: Fri, 16 Feb 1996 02:00:29 -0700
X-Sender: realty@mail.aros.net
To: real-estate@aros.net
From: Mario Giordani <realty@aros.net>
Subject: ** LIST YOUR HOMES FOR FREE **
Sender: owner-real-estate@aros.net
Reply-To: real-estate@aros.net

From The Home Port Realtor's Forum http://www.aros.
net/~realty/

===================

THE HOME PORT NEWS

===================

If you have a home page with your listings and you
would like additional exposure for them, simply use
our newly developed form to add your listings. FREE.

http://www.aros.net/~realty/realty3.html -> Under REAL
ESTATE DIRECTORY

You will be asked for a name and a password to enter
your listings:
name: my pw: listings ——-> small caps only

REQUIREMENTS

1. You MUST have a photo online to point to.
2. You MUST have a Web page.

RULES for FREE listings:

* Listings will be displayed until they are sold
* Entries without photos will be deleted
* You MUST add a link to The Home Port on your page

NO HOME PAGE AND NO SCANNED PHOTOS? Try This…

If you want us to scan a photo of your listing and
display it online for you and your sellers, there is a
nominal $15 quarterly maintenance fee which includes
(1) photo scan. Additional photos are $2.50 each. If
you have a home page with listings and photos, then
this offer is FREE.

* This offer is subject to change without notice and
is experimental.

```
================THE HOME PORT ===================
URL: http://www.aros.net/~realty/realty.html

=====================================================
FORUM: http://www.aros.net/~realty/mailing.html

=====================================================
```

Despite an occasionally posted notice that his is an unmonitored forum, Mario keeps an eye on this group to make sure it remains devoted to a professional discussion of real estate issues. Mario frequently intervenes when certain members dominate discussions with rambling product promotions, long lists of lawyer jokes or diatribes on subjects unrelated to real estate. But because the Home Forum is such a valuable source of contacts and information, most of the discipline on irrelevant contributions comes from the users themselves.

Mario says his biggest frustration, one that many veterans of the earlier stages of the cybernetic revolution share, is "babysitting a mailing list forum for the people who don't know how to unsubscribe." You'll want to do that from time to time, just as you cancel the newspaper when you leave town for a couple of weeks.

LEARNING AS HE GOES

When you call up Charlie Doyle's page, you get RE/MAX balloons again. But this time it's a more developed site, chosen as one of the top ten sites in Massachusetts by *Banker & Tradesman* magazine for January 1996. The button with Charlie's picture brings up a short bio.

Then Charlie makes things as easy as possible for his visitors with three clearly marked hyperlinks:

Determine your price online takes you to the Center for Mobility Resources relocation salary calculator and mortgage qualification calculator.

Tell Charlie what you're looking for provides an email link for you to describe what kind of property you want using a personal home profile questionnaire.

View Charlie's and RE/MAX Prestige Listings takes you to listings matching your profile and preferences.

Very clean and simple. You have to know that most of the buying prospects who come to Charlie after going through this process are serious, well-qualified buyers.

There are links to various useful Web sites, including WebEstate, IRED and—of course —other RE/MAX sites around the world. And

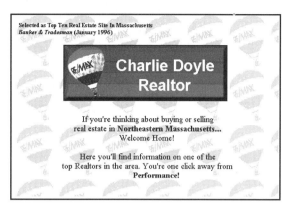

FIGURE 4-8

Charlie Doyle's Real Estate home page (http://www. cdremax.com chas@cdremax.com)

there are related links, such as to Salem Five Cent Savings Bank, which offers virtual banking and "$100 off on mortgage fees to Internet customers only."

So, does this put Charlie light-years ahead of Christy Day and other capable agents who haven't yet gotten up to speed on the Internet? He doesn't think so. He said in a recent email message:

```
Scott,

I must admit that like most of the real estate agents
out there, I am learning as I go along. 6 months ago I
had never even heard of the Web, so when I have
technical problems I get professional help.

A company that my brother works for is doing most of
my web page work. I am overseeing the content and
working on contacts and promoting it. He would be
happy to answer any questions as well: Mike Doyle,
email mike@theeditors.com.
```

It took Charlie several weeks and several hundred dollars to get his original page up. Ever since, he has been adding links and bulking up the information provided on his site. He had his brother add his questionnaire for buyers on the hunch that people would respond to that more than they do to email invitations, though Charlie has a prominent button for email as well as an 800 number.

Charlie's first score off his Web page was rather commonplace: a woman who had misplaced his business card found him on the Internet.

Charlie advises agents with new Web sites to concentrate heavily on information about their market area. "Thinking that putting your site up will get people from around the world to look at it is not realistic," Charlie says. "So aim the page's content toward the potential customers right in your own backyard."

Charlie writes:

> Getting your business on the Internet is not as complicated as you may think. There are many companies that will get you online for as little or as much as you want to spend. In the real estate business we do not buy a printing press and try to print our own brochures, and we do not make our own yard signs. We should not build our own Web pages (unless you are a technical person with experience).
>
> If you are not sure about the larger investment to have a professional site done, hook up with a larger site and they will publish your listings and a photo of you with your phone number for less than it costs to have 1,000 business cards printed. If you have any results at all, take a portion of that money that you made from the results and invest it in the next level of page. Keep building it until you have what you want, then keep building it until you have what the consumer wants. Just like the computer itself, your Web site will be ever-changing.

HOT STUFF

Some of my favorite sites are the simplest, chock full of information and barren of non-essential graphics and multimedia enhancements. But as new sites appear, many of them use more sophisticated multimedia: sound, animation, etc. Here are a couple of possibilities you may want to consider for your own page.

We've already talked about using sound to provide background music and audio tours. If you are doing business on the Pacific rim, it makes sense to use sound to bridge language barriers. MacDonald Realtors of Vancouver (*http://www.rew.bc.ca./140*), the 1994 top independent real estate company in British Columbia, with over half a billion dollars in sales, does just that. To its text translations in Chinese, MacDonald adds RealAudio translations in Japanese. The multilingual multimedia atmosphere of the MacDonald Web pages is more than a gimmick. A company subsidiary, TCD Consultants Ltd., offers immigration and investment advice. TCD maintains a full-time office in Taipei, Taiwan, and works closely with affiliated corporations in Hong Kong, the Philippines, Singapore and the People's

Republic of China. On the investment consulting side, the company employs two Mandarin-speaking MBAs to assist individuals of high net worth in identifying suitable vehicles for immigration to Canada under the "entrepreneur" category.

If you point your mouse at Greg White's face on the Choice One Better Homes and Gardens (*http://real-estate-sales.com/*) home page and click the mouse on his eyes, you will be taken to a page with a row of flashing eyes. "With these eyes," Greg's text promises, "I will find the buyer great value. In addition, these eyes are trained to find qualified buyers for your home." Greg's face is image-mapped to produce that amusing little effect, and the rest of Greg's award-winning pages are rich with information, including a "Reference Room" awash in blue hot buttons taking you to a wealth of data about Seattle-Tacoma real estate.

Chapter 5 The Telecommuting Agent

The wonder of the Internet is that it cares nothing about time and space. It will enable you to do business locally and reach out to extend your sphere of influence far beyond your city limits or county line. This chapter reflects the "think globally, act locally" message of most Web-savvy agents I talked to. They say the Web is a wonderful tool when mastered and reinforced by the best of tried and true methods for getting listings, contacts, referrals, and relocation business.

- ▶ Web Pages Attract Listings
- ▶ The Future Is Now
- ▶ T.J. Saw It Coming
- ▶ Techno-Realty in Missouri
- ▶ The Best Advertising Tool

WEB PAGES ATTRACT LISTINGS

Donald Gares of Creative Farm and Home Realty (*http://www.netins. net/showcase/gares/*) in Keosauqua, Iowa, says, "In my rural area, where the Internet is still in its childhood, it is a far better listing than selling tool. Local individuals are very impressed when they can go to the local library, school, etc., and see their property on a computer screen. It is definitely a super means of listing property."

"All real estate is local." A lot of real estate agents intone that reassuring mantra when talk turns to the subject of the high-powered (and expensive) electronic real estate office. After all, those agents remind themselves, someone in New Jersey who wants to buy a piece of property in Montana eventually has to catch a plane to Montana and find someone who knows Montana real estate.

It's one thing to get a better understanding of the Internet and its tools; it's yet another to start spending time and money to harness all that into your own daily real estate practice. So no matter how much hype agents hear about the Internet and the potential riches of relocation and referral business from distant exotic places, some agents are not going to get interested in the Net until they are convinced that Web page will reach locals.

Many agents have come to realize that to harvest the bounty the Web can bring, you must first become more connected than ever to your local community. You need to know which other businesses and services in your area are online and what they offer. You need to encourage them to exchange links with you. You have to act on electronic "calls to opportunity" as soon as they come your way from all those distant places. What electronic tools like email enable you to do is get the word out instantly that you are the one to introduce out-of-towners to your local real estate market and the charms of your community.

THE FUTURE IS NOW

Not very long ago the vision of the telecommuting office of the near future had little to do with online communication, much less anything like the Internet. As recently as 1994 here's what two otherwise very astute observers had to say about the pipe dream of merged computer technology:

> "In the heavily touted 'office of the future,' everything was going to be integrated into one ball of computer wax. The last time we looked, there

were separate typewriters (now called computers), separate laser printers, separate fax machines, separate copy machines, separate postal meters. The office of the future is aptly named—a concept that will remain ever in the future."[1]

Well, those separate machines (except the postal meter) can now be purchased in a single piece of hardware—with scanner, modem and several other bells and whistles thrown in to boot. That integrated "ball of computer wax" may not be to everyone's taste, but versions of it hit the retail shelves shortly after the words above were written.

(Al and Jack's book, by the way, is a wise, entertaining—and short—book to read before you design or redesign your Web site.)

Where is all this technology heading? And for those of us who are not independently wealthy already, where will it all end? How far should you get technologically out in front of your business peers and potential customers since you still have to do business with them in a way that makes them comfortable and fits the everyday realities of your community? After all, it doesn't do you much good to have a 28.8 mhz modem if local phone lines won't transmit faster than 19.2.

PERSONAL ACCOUNT

T. J. Anderson
Internet Media Works
http://www.inetworks.com
tja@bga.com

T. J. Saw it Coming

Some people have been mastering the electronic tools of the trade and finding solutions to technical problems for a long time. These successful players don't give themselves the option of throwing up their hands and walking away in disgust when valuable communications equipment doesn't function. All real estate may be local, but the "do-it-now" pace required of telecommuting agents means you have to be ready to respond quickly to referrals and requests for information about your community and local real estate market.

It hardly comes as a surprise that the people who know and use the tools of the telecommuting real estate agent also know one another. As I spoke with other connected agents, several pointed me in the direction of commercial broker T. J. Anderson in Austin, Texas.

T. J. is what technology marketers calls "an early adopter." She's been involved for years in spreading the computer revolution:

About 15 years ago, I recognized that computerized real estate offices would be the wave of the future. At that time, I owned a commercial real estate firm. CPM and the first Apple computers were just evolving into usable media. As we all remember, they were large and cumbersome, with

---

[1] Al Ries and Jack Trout, *The 22 Immutable Laws of Marketing*

limited software. But I recognized the potential and set about designing on paper the virtual real estate office I wanted to have. Eventually.

Needless to say, at that time I had never heard of the Internet. While still dreaming of the virtual real estate community, I recognized in some of the newer BBS systems (which by the '90s had become graphically based) the potential to at least partially meet my needs. A discussion with one of my tenants turned me on to the Internet.

In late 1993 I sold a house to a woman who headed up a state agency on information services. That buyer introduced me to Mosaic, and my world turned around overnight. I had found the way to realize my dreams of a virtual real estate community.

Mosaic
The first browser for the World Wide Web that supported hypermedia.

For T. J., the hard part was getting other agents as excited as she was about the Internet. Few people believed the future she envisioned would merge with the present so quickly, that title companies and other real estate service providers would be scrambling so fast to offer their services on the Internet.

My plan was to bring together all real estate-related entities in Austin and surrounding communities via the Internet and World Wide Web. I envisioned all real estate agents, title companies, lenders and affiliated service providers having email and providing information via the Internet to the real estate community as well as to the general public.

For instance, a title company and a brokerage could easily connect with buyer and seller to conduct a transaction via the Internet. An agent could schedule a closing and forward a contract to the title company by email, sending a copy to the lender, appraiser and all persons involved with one broadcast email. This leaves the perfect "paper trail" (without the paper)

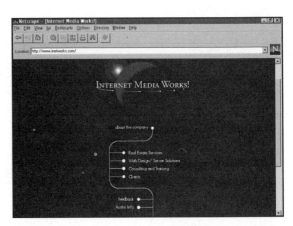

FIGURE 5-1
Internet Media Works home page design, hosting and consulting services (http://www. inctworks,com)

that all parties need to keep on file. I envision a totally internetworked system where in the not-too-distant future most real estate transactions can be completed via the Internet.

We are totally reliant upon the fax machine for this purpose today, but this requires paper and long distance charges and the constant frustration of busy signals. With email or other basic Internet capabilities, all of these negative things are removed.

You didn't notice T. J. talking about buyers from London or Singapore buying investment property in Texas, or convincing investors in New Orleans or Dallas to build or buy offices in Austin. Though a nationally known expert on real estate uses of the Internet, she concentrated first on trying to establish the technological means to make local Austin real estate transactions work better.

TECHNO-REALTY IN MISSOURI

I discovered Marilyn and Larry Daniel's Web page because it was linked to Bill Hutchinson's. The two were too geographically separated (one in Missouri, the other in Alaska) to be competitors and had struck up a relationship swapping Web page tips and techniques.

The Daniels' page definitely belongs to the "nothing fancy" school. It's clean and simple, but everything that counts is right there. Scrolling down the page, you get frequent email invitations and buttons to other pages, including résumés. Most important, the Daniels wisely and clearly explain who they are, highlighting Marilyn's 17 years experience as a Springfield school teacher, Larry's three years in real estate and 22 years heading the Daniel Trucking Company, as well as his having attended the Harvard Graduate School of Business. You're told that these are not just two real estate agents, but a couple with rich and varied lives.

A link to the ORION site takes you to the Ozarks Regional Information Online Network, a community information network for southwest Missouri "with its initial modem pool being located in Springfield, and its servers located in Columbia." Larry was one of the volunteer Web page designers for ORION.

Linking to ORION covered a lot of bases for the Daniels. The site has links to Springfield public schools, the Springfield-Greene County Library, local newsgroups and electronic mail providers, and various community resources such as health care, business resources,

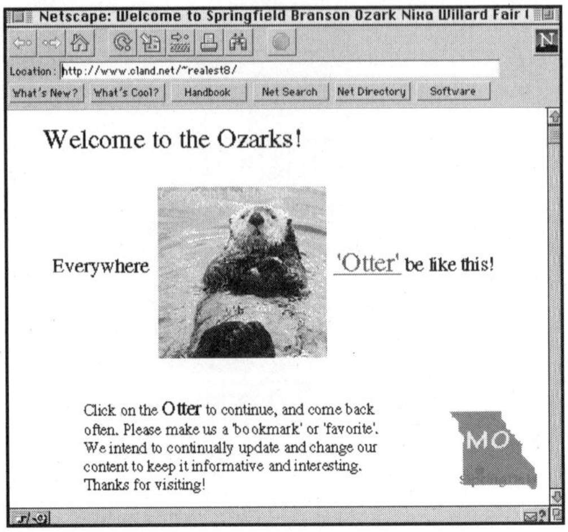

FIGURE 5-2

Larry and Marilyn Daniel's home page (http://www.cland. net/~realest8/)

internet resources, the senior center, teen center, and local history and recreation.

There is a valuable lesson here: don't waste your time and limited resources reinventing the wheel. You can almost bet that there a number of sites within your local area and community, maintained by the chamber of commerce, schools, and nonprofits, that you can simply build a link to from your site. When you do that, you give extensive local information to your visitors, and all it costs you is a half dozen keystrokes of coding.

The Daniels' Web site has a one-thing-after-another sturdy patchwork quilt design, but it has up-to-date tools, including a link from Matchpoint for their listings. Matchpoint (*http://www.arsdata.com/mp*) allows home seekers to fill out a questionnaire specifying geographical area, price, number of bedrooms, etc., and then be taken directly to listing pages on agents' sites.

The Daniels' Web site leverages the influential role they have attained in their community. Larry observes:

Of course, being involved in the business community through the local chamber of commerce for many years, including serving on their board of directors, has been a help in the real estate business as well. There's no question that our strong contacts with local bankers and business people have helped us. Certainly you cannot abuse the access, but when it is necessary it certainly helps to have the name recognition and personal acquaintance that gets you past the secretary.

Among the agents who were early adopters of the Net there has developed a kind of informal "each one teach one" spirit, and Larry has helped other companies set up their first pages. Marilyn, a local Easter Seal Society director, volunteered Larry's services to help the Society create a Web home page "to make a whole new audience aware of the services we provide."

That altruism has another benefit for Larry: he now has a fledgling Web consulting business. "There is a natural progression from HTML authoring and Web page indexing right into Internet consulting," said Larry. "It is really exciting to get involved in a project early on and help people avoid the potholes that await the unwary."

PERSONAL ACCOUNT

**Marilyn Daniel
Keller Williams Realty**
http://www.cland. net/~realest8

ldaniel@mail.orion.org

A Day in the Life

The ability to telecommute has not handed the Daniels a life of leisure. It's just made them more efficient. Telecommuting tools simply allow agents to juggle more projects and deals at one time. Marilyn describes a typical day:

7:00 AM While Larry is downloading the overnight changes in the MLS distributed system to our desktop and two laptop computers, he also goes online to check the email.

8:00 AM We review and reply to the overnight email inquiries from our web page, go over the day's schedule, and prepare the files and proposals we will need that day.

9:00 AM I meet with a prospective first-time homebuyer in one of the conference rooms at the real estate office and begin the interview and educational process with the information packet we have prepared. After explaining the benefits of being prequalified, I put the buyer on the phone with a lender. Larry uses one of the laptops to run a presentation to explain seller, buyer, and disclosed dual agency.

11:00 AM I get a call from a lady in California Larry had been emailing. She was very appreciative of the information and timely responses she had gotten. She and her husband were nearing retirement from the military and were considering moving to southwest Missouri. They had considered other areas, but were unsuccessful in obtaining information from other contacts they had made through the Internet. I told her Larry would email her some names of lenders that do VA financing. Then she talked with Larry when he came back in the office after completing a commercial sale earlier that morning. They talked about where VA pharmacies were located, and Larry told her he would check with some military contacts and email her the information. She indicated she would like a lender to call her, and we told her we would arrange for one of the loan representatives we work with quite often and successfully to give her a call.

I had previously sent her one of our packets for out of state potential buyers which included a local Homes magazine. Larry told her how to email her property selections information so that he could email back more info about the properties.

12:30 PM I finished up the paperwork for a closing we had scheduled for that afternoon, a sale we had made as the result of having the property on our Web page. A couple from Virginia had purchased it a month or so ago while visiting relatives in Missouri. They intend to retire here in a few years and while cruising the Web had viewed our page and contacted us for help in finding some land to build on when they retire.

4:00 PM Larry and I met with the sellers at the closing company. After a short visit we went into the conference room to get signatures on the road agreement and covenants for the development. We finished the closing about 5:00 PM and went home.

7:00 PM After supper Larry checked his email and read a message from some potential buyers in Kansas who had been looking for a place near one of our many lakes. He had sent them email the previous night about a property he had found through another agent he had met while holding an open house the previous Sunday. She had mailed him three computer printouts with photos and one of them met the parameters. Larry had sent a brief description to them to see if they wanted us to fax them the sheet. We faxed it to them, and they were really interested. They asked to have a lender call them so that when they visit the property we will be able to tell the seller they are prequalified if they decide to make an offer.

Larry paged one of the loan officers we work with to call us. In about ten minutes she called, and we gave her the number in Kansas and sent them an email to let them know she would be calling. While online sending this email, we got another email from them wanting to know when we would be available to show them the property. While answering this email we got the call back from the lender telling us it appeared the potential buyers were in a good position to be approved, either for the home with 20 acres or even the home and 40 acres which was offered as an alternative. Larry proceeded to finish the email, which also included an explanation of seller and buyer agency, and sent it with a tentative appointment to show the property the weekend after next.

8:00 PM We drove to the post office to send off some information packets to other contacts from the Internet, one from Juneau, Alaska, who is investigating a possible transfer to Springfield. Then we went to buy some plastic adhesive runners for an upcoming open house. Back home, Larry got back on the computer to reply to any other email and complete a Homes ad in Adobe Pagemaker 6.0 so it will appear the way we want it to instead of having to try to communicate to the printer what we want. By now it is after 10:00 PM and nearing the time to call it another day in this exciting and increasingly Internet and email-oriented business!

ROAD WARRIOR GEAR

So what do you actually need to go to work as a telecommuting real estate agent? If you are convinced that you want to catch up with T.J. Anderson and Larry Daniel, what's the fastest way to get up to speed? Here's Larry's formula:

I would suggest getting the best laptop you can afford, a Pentium with a one gigabyte or larger hard drive, 28.8 PC Card modem, CD-ROM, Windows 95, and Internet Explorer (or Netscape). If your local MLS has a distributed or downloadable system, load that on your laptop, too. This is especially true if they offer downloadable color photos of listings. With this and some of the popular real estate software packages that are available like Top Producer, you will be set up to show potential clients and customers what is currently on the market, what has sold, what didn't sell, and, depending on the MLS's software system, very likely some statistics and other information.

You'll be able to update your database online to catch the very latest listings from the MLS. You can also cruise the Web for other information such as current mortgage rates and information on other cities that a client may be relocating to. (I am expecting that, before long, insurance agencies will be coming to the Internet with at least ballpark insurance quotes.) And you'll be able to maintain and update your own Web pages.

With a presentation package like Microsoft's Powerpoint, it is easy to do on-screen presentations for listing presentations and other tools to assist you with obtaining additional business. We have one on buyer agency that really helps us explain the concept.

To complete the package, you will need a way to connect your laptop to your desktop computer so you can keep all your files concurrent. This can be done fairly inexpensively through Lap-Link or PCAnywhere software. Networking calls for more computer knowledge, offers more flexibility with printing, and normally costs more. If your office is large enough to require a network, it will need a network administrator to get you connected.

Larry says that there's no question that a good Web page is a key part of the telecommuting mix. It brings additional business that would be very difficult and expensive to obtain otherwise.

No agent can afford to advertise everywhere. At this stage of the Internet, it isn't that powerful a listing tool. But soon "Do you have a

Web page?" will be one of the first five questions a listing prospect asks. And a Web page can help create favorable comments about you in the community. It pleases me when someone comes up to us at a community event and says, "I saw your page on the Web last week." What a perfect opportunity to talk real estate!

If you want to make your Web page an even more powerful tool in your local bailiwick, Ray Dixon of WebEstate offers a reminder that by making local copies of your *jpgs*, *gifs* and *html* files (or having your computer guru do it for you) you can display your Web page on an office computer so that when prospective buyers and sellers walk into your office, they can browse what you have to offer while they are there.

PERSONAL ACCOUNT

Rich Czeh
Realty Executives
http://www.infinet. com/~richac
richac@infinet.com

The Best Advertising Tool

Real estate agent Rich Czeh, of Columbus, Ohio, became a fan of both the Net and telecommuting early on:

Telecommuting agents need to make intensive use of computers and programs that will make excellent presentations, that raise the ante on presenting a more professional image of themselves and their services to the buying public. I have a Web site. Most agents in my area don't, and they know I can market to a larger audience.

For relocation customers, I send out a package with a hard copy of the material I sent them electronically. I send out some update info weekly and a short email message to let them know I'm still alive.

In the email (which is often out within half an hour of receiving their request) I include properties that would be of interest to them, as well as school district information.

As far as working from your home as a telecommuting agent, providing top-notch service from home is not the problem. The problem is not knowing how the client, who doesn't know you or your organization, will perceive you. I think until the client feels comfortable with your expertise, a larger visible business office may lend itself to creating a greater feeling of

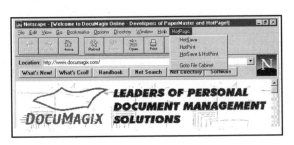

FIGURE 5-3
"Documagix Hot Page" (http://www. documagix.com)

security. But fast, efficient, accurate, friendly service is the main thing, whether you provide it from home or an office.

I have always enjoyed tinkering on computers and wanted to include my business in my enjoyment of computers. It also seemed that the Net would be a vast market and couldn't be ignored. I felt that to use commercial sites would be unaffordably expensive, and I thought I could do a better job myself anyway. Also, when people access my site, I don't pay for built-in competition.

My site has definitely drawn buyers. I had people contacting me instead of my having to find them.

Learning to code and trying to make my page look as professional as I could was frustrating at first. But doing it myself gave me the feeling of being able to create something that works and something most other agents are afraid to try. It's an especially good feeling when someone tells my how nice the site is.

My first Web page cost me about $40—for the program and book. It took me about three days, full time. I presently spend about four hours weekly updating, and numerous hours trying different things and searching for things to try to keep my page interesting. I still haven't got it right, but it is working for me. Once buyers or sellers contact me (if I do my job right), there is no competition.

6 Give in Order to Get

In January 1996, Netscape began selling Netscape 2.0, after giving away millions of free copies of its earlier version. Then they started letting people use Netscape 3.0 for free. Everyone striving to make a living on the Web seems to spend big chunks of energy giving things away as fast as they can. This chapter will explore why they do that.

▶ Cast Your Bread

▶ What's in It for You

▶ Teach Your Customers How to Shop You

▶ The Net Incites Interaction

CAST YOUR BREAD

Giving things away on the Net, especially ideas and information, is more than a marketing ploy. It's a deeply imbedded part of Internet culture that stems from its academic and scientific origins. The Internet evolved, after all, in order to allow people to share databanks and pursue cooperative projects. And taxpayers originally paid for most of the early Internet.

When she first began to explore the marketing possibilities of the Internet, says T.J. Anderson, "it seemed the 'Net community' was in denial that their 'baby' could be overrun with commercialization. I had no real idea of how to make money on the Net," she recalls, "I just knew it was the place to be and where the world would be in years to come."

As academic uses gave way to recreational surfing and the use of the Internet as an exciting new way for ordinary people to communicate over vast distances, that anti-commercial spirit gave way only grudgingly. The second wave of early users went to the Internet for amusement—and to get things for free.

So how do you make money on the Net when its users so easily balk at the notion of paying for things?

First of all, making sales is not the only reward for you on the Net. Casting your bread upon the waters can be rewarding in itself. People like T.J. Anderson, Larry Daniel and Bill Hutchinson all have gained enormously from the time they invested swapping ideas and knowledge with others about the Net. Those kind enough to give Net newcomers advice and guidance have come to be called Net angels, and that kind of virtue does offer its own rewards.

But real estate salespeople tend to squirm and look for the exit when they hear talk like that. Everyone wants a free piece of an agent's time. No group is more besieged than real estate agents with pleas to volunteer for this and flip hamburgers for that. A hundred volunteer outings down the line agents lose their shyness about asking, "What's in it for me?"

WHAT'S IN IT FOR YOU

Like Fuller Brush salespeople going from door to door handing out vegetable brushes and soap samples, Net marketers give away freebies: free information, free software, free space to post real estate listings. They do that for the same reason you offer a free competitive market analysis to every homeowner you know who mentions the possibility of selling. You may give those things away partly out of altruism; you certainly give them away out of enlightened self-interest.

Those of you who farm neighborhoods the old-fashioned way would never think of going from door to door without bringing things to hand out—pens, notepads, pot holders, and refrigerator magnets—door openers to get you a friendly reception and an occasional invitation inside for a cup of coffee and a chance to develop a rewarding relationship.

Like the mailmerge program that allows you to farm from a computer database, a Web site can save you a lot of shoe leather. Walking door to door like a letter carrier is good exercise, but when you figure in your time, isn't it cheaper to post a billboard on the fastest growing highway in the world and give away free things only to those who contact you and ask for them? When you think of it that way, making sure you have plenty of free help to offer, plenty of attractive relocation packages, plenty of informative brochures and complementary newsletters, is a small price to pay to cultivate the contacts you generate through the Net.

Your Web site and the hard copy materials you use for follow-up are your opportunities to educate prospects—and existing clients as well—about what you do and how well you do it. Once your page is up, it's easy to update it to tell the world about new skills and resources you have that your competition may not be able to match.

TEACH YOUR CUSTOMERS HOW TO SHOP YOU

As a successful loan broker I know likes to put it, "If you're any good, you teach your customers how to shop you." Shopping you is what potential customers do when, having heard what you have to offer, they go out to see whether the next agent may offer even more. Teaching them how to shop you works best if you give prospects a point-by-point scorecard. That card, often presented as a list of questions, serves as a checklist of all the services and benefits you offer that your competitors do not. The time—and Web page space—you spend educating potential customers about ways to meet their needs is your chance to help them recognize the components of superior service and come back to you when they are ready to buy.

They'll come back if you have given them memorable reasons to do so. People at a dance tend to feel comfortable dancing with the one who showed them how to do the steps. If you are the one who taught a couple what "amortizes" means, and showed them why signing up for a 30-year mortgage and making double payments is smarter than committing themselves to a 15-year mortgage, if you are the kind of agent to unveil hazards and opportunities others don't, people will trust you and come back your way. They will even pass out your business cards and brag to their friends about your Web page.

PERSONAL ACCOUNT

Ira and Carol Serkes, CRS, GRI

Berkeley RE/MAX Realtor

http://www. home-buy-sell.com/Realtor

Realtor@home-buy-sell. com

Making Connections

RE/MAX agents Ira and Carol Serkes know how to create the paths that bring customers back to their door by giving them something to remember. Ira, a published Nolo Press author, freely gives advice to other agents. That habit of generosity, coupled with his proven ability to communicate his expertise, means that—like T.J. and Larry—he has reached the point where he can also now generate income from seminars and consulting. "I enjoy helping others become 'digital'," he says.

Ira admits that when he first built his page he did it as an exclusive forum for promoting his own listings:

> In keeping with the spirit of the Internet, we've now changed to an open site, linking as many real estate listings as possible. I've searched through local real estate office sites to find the URLs where their properties are listed. This gives the surfer instant access to other properties rather than having to surf through lots of my competitors' Web pages. Before they go to my competitors' pages, though, I tell them the benefits of buyer broker-age and remind them that they'll receive the best representation when they hire us.
>
> I include our URL on our business cards, all flyers, open house ads, and email. I've made a sign rider for our For Sale signs so people with Web access know they can reach us immediately.
>
> We've sent out a mailing to about 3,500 people in our database—past clients, neighbors in our "farm," attorneys, CPAs, newspaper and TV reporters.
>
> We also give out AOL and CompuServe disks, free for the asking, at our open houses. We add a sticker with our name, email and Web page addresses. Both AOL and CompuServe offer new users free trial periods.
>
> I registered our site with Yahoo, Netscape, and with another search engine called Submit It! (*http://www.submit-it.com/*), which takes the information and distributes it to many other search engines.
>
> We cross-link our site to as many places as possible. I have several links to local radio stations, and they have our URL on their listeners' Web site. We've linked our site with the city of Berkeley, and they've linked our site to

their business page. Anyone looking at Berkeley's Web site will be able to find us. We've also registered our site with CAR, the California Association of Realtors. We're always looking for other local businesses or organizations to link to.[2]

The first thing you see when you call up Ira and Carol's page is a notice in stark black print: "Serkes Berkeley Real Estate Search Engine, Realtor, CRS—RE/MAX Referrals." Then, while a color photo of a railroad engine comes into focus, you learn that the engine pictured is "Union Pacific 3985 Challenger on Altamont Pass."

What follows immediately is a notice that:

"We respect the value of your time."

"This site is optimized for speed, not fancy graphics!"

Next, Ira plugs his book *How to Buy a House in California,* which has "already helped over 36,000 California home buyers!"

Train-loving whimsy to provoke your curiosity, no time-wasting graphics, agents who wrote the book on buying houses…it all adds up to a varied invitation to spend more time at the Serkes' site.

Ira and Carol include a link to a section entitled "Qualities to Demand in Your Realtor," which offers laudatory letters from happy customers grouped under hypertexted heads as:

Integrity, market knowledge & real estate expertise

Personal attention & service

Thoroughness & attention to details

Someone who succeeds when other agents have failed

An agent who contributes back to the real estate industry

Call it shameless self-promotion if you will, but reprinting letters of endorsement is a time-tested marketing tool. Endorsements are a tangible way for prospects to judge someone they've never met.

PERSONAL ACCOUNT

**Gary Gooley
Blackburn & Co.
Real Estate**
*http://www.stlweb.com/
blackburn/2020.html*
grcool@mtnhome.com

20/20 Shopping Plan

Arkansas sales agent Gary Cooley gives his Web visitors outstanding information about his area, extensive access to local resources, and even a greeting from the mayor of Mountain Home. Then, to tell buyers exactly what he asks of them before they move on to see what the next agent has to say on the next Web page, he offers:

[2] © Copyright 1995. *Used with permission from Ira Serkes.*

Gary Cooley

Coming to the Mountain Home area to look at real estate? Do it the fast, easy way. Use my 20/20 Buyer's Program. The goal of the program is for me to locate your new home or land within 20 hours or 20 showings. That's where the "20/20" comes from. There's no cost to you. I don't use high pressure, tricky, or slick sales tactics. I have no need of resorting to such acts. Like this Web site, all I do is present information. Here's how it works.

The Clear Vision comes from listening to your interests and needs. All I need is for you to explain your interests to me as we tour the area. I then apply my area knowledge to your needs and we go from there. It is that simple. All the market information you just read is applied to your needs. With rare exceptions I'm able to locate what my buyers want within that 20 hours or 20 showings goal.

Why work this way? I've found that many people come to look while on vacation or over a long weekend. They don't have a great deal of time. Others come back and look a little bit each year while on vacation. It may take two or three years for them to find what they want. If they only look at four or five homes each year it takes a few years to find the right place. Ultimately most people do spend about 20 hours or look at about 20 properties before deciding on one place.

What's in this for me? Time! My greatest challenge in my real estate career is time management. You help me with my challenges, I'll help you with yours. All I ask is that you work with me for those 20 showings or 20 hours, whichever comes first. If you keep switching from real estate agent to real estate agent, you create problems for both of us. I'll not be able to devote my time to you because I've got to spend my time wisely. It is not in your best interest to keep switching agents, whether you work with me or any other agent. Here's why.

When you start looking for a home in this area you probably won't have a great deal of time. If you switch from agent to agent you'll create several problems for yourself. First of all, each agent will need to know what you want so you'll end up explaining yourself over and over. That takes time and takes your attention away from progressing with the search. Next, you'll have to keep a list of what you have seen, and tell each agent what you have already seen, so that you don't waste time looking at the same places twice. Again, that's a bunch of wasted time. Further, you'll have to explain to each agent what you did and did not like about the places you've already seen. Any agent who works on anything besides high pressure tactics needs this kind of feedback. That takes even more time.

By working with one agent, that agent quickly learns your likes and dislikes. You'll save yourself a lot of time and frustration.

I'll bet that when the time comes for most buyers to go out and "shop" Gary, he has them happily in escrow.

THE NET INCITES INTERACTION

Before we go on to talk about building Web sites, I want to reinforce something Michael Russer said earlier. The Internet is not simply a form of technology; it is a new way of communicating, a fundamental shift in the way people relate to one another. Increasing interactivity is the point of most new Web software products and technology: to induce visitors to linger at a Web site long enough to build a relationship that can lead to a genuine transaction.

The spirit of the Internet can strengthen people's active resourcefulness in related areas. For instance, we are hearing stories of landlords installing ISDN lines in their apartment buildings and offering free online classes to fill vacant units.

Similarly, Tom Lynch, a Sonoma County, California, contractor, purchased a former tavern and pizza parlor in semi-derelict condition on the banks of the Russian River and managed to attract investors and office tenants by installing four T-1 lines to create The Internet Cafe (*http://www.on-the-river.com*). Tom offers a full Internet Service Provider 24 hours a day for tables furnished with eight Internet-capable Pentium 120s with VG100 lines from the computers direct to the service provider. "When I let it be known that I was going to do an Internet cafe, the investors and tenants appeared," Tom says.

Getting more involved in the Internet means that you will have many opportunities to show customers and clients how they in turn can leverage the impact of the Net to increase the value of their real estate investments.

Whether we're talking about interactivity technology for the Web (discussion forums, questionnaires, scrollable frames, free calendar space, etc.) or of broader applications of the marketing principal behind those devices, the lessons are the same: make the most active use of communication technology; give something to get something; add value to make your business grow.

7 To Build or Not to Build Your Own Web Site

As we have examined the Internet and seen what other real estate agents have done with their Web sites, the question lurking for most of you has probably been, "How and when should I build a Web page of my own?" The next chapters will focus on that question.

▶ Local Boy Makes Web Site

▶ Roll Your Own

▶ Go Slow

▶ If You Don't Have the Time and Energy…

LOCAL BOY
MAKES WEB SITE

When Tom Cuneo, manager of the Sebastopol, California, office of Frank Howard Allen real estate, wanted an improved faster-loading home page for the office Web site, he turned to Emmett Dzieza. A science and art student as well as a competitive swimmer, Emmett tinkers with his own Web page in his spare time (*http://www.sonic. net/~edzieza*).

Emmett's father Bruce has Willow Creek Financial downstairs from Tom's office. So when Tom mentioned to Bruce that he felt he was in over his head and needed help improving his home page, Emmett's name came up. The only thing remarkable about the realty office putting its Web fortunes in Emmett's hands is that Emmett was fifteen years old at the time.

"Hey, those kids know a lot more about the Web than I do," Tom says. "I had just barely started surfing the Net at that point."

The country is full of Emmetts, bright, inquisitive young men and women who take as naturally to Web page design as earlier generations did to hot rods or rock guitars. With little money and even less experience, some of the pages these kids design are among the most intriguing and innovative on the Net.

All Tom knew about the Net was that he wanted a presence there that would attract business. Tom hired Emmett to build his pages. Maybe he couldn't talk Emmett's language, but Tom didn't surf with his eyes closed either. When he saw Web home pages with simple graphics on smartly appealing watermark backgrounds that came up quickly, he didn't hesitate to ask fifteen-year-old Emmett if he knew how to create pages like that. Emmett certainly did.

So building a Web page is simple, right? A fifteen-year-old can do it. With a few high school kids and an empty garage you could start a Web site assembly line. You may not go that far, but if you are not interested in learning how to build your own Web pages, and don't have a budget that permits hiring a professional design company, don't despair. Your local high school or junior college can be a rich and affordable source of expertise and labor.

ROLL YOUR OWN

Bank of America vice president Karen Shapiro, product manager for the company's interactive marketing unit, told me 75–80 percent of the design and content for the B of A Web pages was done in-house, with outside vendors providing page layout and HTML. Of course, "in-house" at Bank of America, with all its resources, is probably a little different than "in-house" at your business.

You're the best judge of whether it's wiser to hire someone or build your own page. You have to ask yourself just how much time and energy you want to put into this rapidly changing art form. Are you up to mastering the latest Java or Shockwave applets, and multiple scrollable frames? Can you get the vision you have for your page to actually function or will it be one of the Web sites people visit only once because it disappoints?

PERSONAL ACCOUNT

Larry Daniel
http://www.clad.net/
~realest8.html

realest8@worldnet.att.net

Accessing the Real Costs

Larry Daniel points out that to do it well yourself means making an open-ended time commitment that actually may cost you money. To assess the real cost, pay yourself something for work hours invested, including the hours spent surfing the Web to get ideas and see what other HTML authors are doing.

Larry calculates that he spent several hundred hours doing just that before he started working on his own page. He says he spent $6,500 for a faster Pentium machine complete with sound and a 17-inch monitor, $250 for a 28.8 modem, $49.95 a month for a local Internet business account, $600 for Adobe Photoshop (so he could work with images and art), $39 for Netscape, $50 for MS Plus (to get MS Internet Explorer).

Larry's costs would be typical for a small non-networked office setup, though he obviously indulged himself on the computer. A perfectly acceptable Pentium 100, with a 1-gigabyte hard drive and a decent monitor can be had for $2,500.

Larry is also equipped to create and process the photos he and Marilyn use on their pages:

> For images for the Web pages I use some or all of the following equipment and software in some combination: Adobe Photoshop 3.0.5 gets a real workout enhancing, sizing, and converting to either *.gif*, *.jpeg*, or the newer transparent *.gif* files. It also works pretty well in producing graphics with text.
>
> We usually take photographs with a Nikon N90 using various lenses with focal lengths varying from 20mm extreme wide angle (which is really good for homes and interiors) to 300mm (that works well for homes near a body of water).
>
> I have an older 486 33mhz computer with a Microtek Scanmaker 600Z flatbed scanner for converting photographs and/or artwork to *.tiff* files (and

occasionally other file formats) and save them to diskette. Then I put the diskette into the Gateway 2000 Pentium 100mhz where I have Photo-shop to edit a file and convert it to *.gif* or *.jpeg*. The Pentium also has CorelDraw 3.0 which is used for developing logos and other images which are also converted with Photoshop.

Just recently I purchased a Polaroid Sprintscan to reduce the need to keep photographs. With it I will be able to scan the negative right onto the Pentium 100 mhz and also not have to worry about sending the last print off for use in one of the advertisements we run on properties we have for sale.

CHECK YOUR NEW PAGES OUT

You'll want to take a look at your newly created Web pages. Larry Daniel reminds you how:

Before you upload a page to your service provider's server, you can try it out with your own browser on your own computer. That may save you em-barrassment (and probably even some time if you are not truly proficient at HTML).

To check the HTML, all you need to do is start your browser of choice and instead of going online simply select the HTML file you want and let the browser load it. The images probably won't load unless they are in the cache from a previous online connection, but you at least are able to make sure the text displays as you want it.

If you really want or need to check the layout complete with images, that takes some more work. Go through the HTML document and replace the image *http://www.wherever.com/~name/filename.gif* or *.jpeg* with *file:///c:\directory\filename.gif* or whatever extension the image file has. Of course, you need to use the correct drive\directory\filename, and when you get all of this done correctly the images and the HTML will load and be viewable in the browser. Some browsers have an Open File option right on the dropdown under the File menu bar; others get you to the Open File option after you select File/Open.

Some editors offer a global replace function which makes the changing back and forth from *http://etc.* to *file:///etc.* quicker and easier. As long as the HTML document isn't too long or doesn't have lots of images I certainly recommend checking the files before uploading them to the server. If it is a really long or image-laden document you can always copy the portion you are changing, add the HTML tags before and after the segment, and check only the edited portion.

Everyone says experience is the best teacher. The experience of up-loading a bad HTML document one night about 11:30 PM taught me to always check mine. I fortunately took enough extra time to check it on the server and found it displayed in such a manner that it was unreadable. Unfortunately it was about two hours later before I had it corrected and finally got to bed. Something as simple as leaving out a quotation mark or a less than sign (<) can totally disrupt the intended display of an HTML document or Web page. Check them out!

A small real estate office could build a completely equipped Web site production and maintenance operation for well under $5,000. And remember, the computer is there for other work besides the Internet. In fact, most real estate offices can probably upgrade their existing PCs for a few hundred dollars and be ready to go.

However, the learning process to keep your home page up with the Joneses never stops. "I am still learning about the World Wide Web," Larry says, "and the browser software keeps changing and improving. It is a constant task to keep it up to date with properties selling and new ones being listed for sale that have to be put up as soon as possible. And just putting up a page is not all that needs to be done. Someone has to know how to get it up on the indices and search engines so that the public has a chance to find it!"

CAVEAT EMPTOR

Larry, despite his own fascination with the workings of the Web and his willingness to keep at building his page, is no particular advocate of the do-it-yourself approach. But he is suspicious of many of the so-called experts offering to build and manage Web sites for a fee:

> If you don't have the time, knowledge, or inclination to do it yourself (as most agents won't), proceed cautiously! There are too many so-called "content" or "service" providers that will tell you just enough to start getting your money. They offer you a deal you can't refuse and don't tell you how limited their services are unless you want to spend even more money (by the hour) for the constant updating that a page requires.
>
> And don't totally delegate the page to anyone not familiar with the real estate laws in your state. At a minimum, review everything before it is put up on the Web so that you are not inadvertently in violation of your state's real estate laws and/or regulations.
>
> Start small. Get a presence—an email account—find out your true costs, and see how it progresses. Try to spend a lot of time surfing the Web. You may not like the service your provider gives. It may be too hard to get online when you want to because some of the unlimited access providers do not have enough modems and it is almost impossible to get connected during the evenings or after school is out. I have at least three ways I can

access the Internet so I can check my email and double-check my page to make sure it is current and all the links are still active.

Above all, get a definite date as to when you will be able to view what a provider puts up for you. Some of them will take your money and then you wait months before anything goes live.

One of the common pitfalls is the membership or subscription to a supposedly elite service/content provider. They contact you to offer an "exclusive" opportunity to participate in a "select" group that is being formed as an index of pages on the Web that they will create and maintain for you. They tell you that "for only x amount of dollars" you can be included in this special Web site which will be promoted and advertised on the Web and will become "the most prominent place for homeshoppers to visit to find their next home" or some such grandiose promise! These fly-by-night promoters are long on promises and short on delivery. Insist on being able to see the pages they are promoting on a live connection; contact some of the current members to ask about results.

PERSONAL ACCOUNT

Sean's Excellent Adventure

**Sean Broderick
Broderick & Associates**
*http://www.
broderick-realty.com/*
sean@intnet.net

In December 1994, Sean Broderick was trying to figure out what to buy his family for Christmas. In the process of looking at computers, a friend gave him his first look at the Internet. The possibilities made Sean's head spin. He saw clearly how his real estate business could benefit from this new gizmo. But as with so many newbies, Sean's journey and his troubles were just beginning:

I was ready to go. All I needed to know was how and where to start.

I tried desperately to figure out how to get on the Web. I contacted local service providers and found many of them were as new to this exploding interactive media as I was. So, where did I go? I went to the source, the Net, for help to find out how to utilize this newly found resource. I hooked up with a local provider and got a cheap shell account.

Now the problem was figuring out how to get onto the graphical side of the Net through the Web. I was staying up later and later sending email to everyone I could find—which, by the way, is the most powerful component of the Net—the ability to access a tremendous amount of information and resources in a short period of time. Finally somebody told me about a site with a downloadable program called TIA (The Internet Adapter). I paid the small license fee, set up the pseudo-slip connection for $25 and, voila, I was on the Web with the help of the downloaded Netscape browser program. My sleep was history.

The next thing I wanted to know was, how could I put pictures of my listings up? I checked Yahoo and other sources on real estate sites. They've grown exponentially now, but at the time there weren't that many good real estate sites or databases. But with the few I pulled up, I was able to emulate their home page design. Of course the quickest way to do that was to copy their source code. By selecting View Source, you can see the code used. Then you can save this code to a file on your hard drive. (This is legal since HTML codes are not proprietary. But don't use other people's artwork or copy. Those are protected.)

Once I read the code I was able to create my own home page by learning from the examples of others. An additional bonus was the fact that once you've created a page you can learn by trial and error the best use of code in a particular instance. And if you don't like it, change it.

The next hurdle was to find a server to put my listings on. I checked around for ISPs that would let me input my listings whenever I wanted (very important) and give me enough space to put all the photos on as well. Photos are the largest space eater on the server, and I needed enough space to hold many images of the same property as well as creating additional pages for new listings as they came in. I found what I was looking for in a server at *www.ftech.net*. For about $40/month they allowed me 15 megabytes of server space and the ability to FTP (file transfer protocol) my information back and forth between my computer and my server at any time (just like the broker load MLS we use in the St. Petersburg Board of Realtors).

Inputting text into HTML language by trial and error is the easiest, but most time-consuming, part of the process. Once you've created the images, text and layout, it's time to view it, test it and rework the pages as many times as it takes to "get it right." I downloaded programs from various sites on the Net to help me educate myself on the programming and layout (e.g., Hotdog, HTML Assistant and GNNPress)

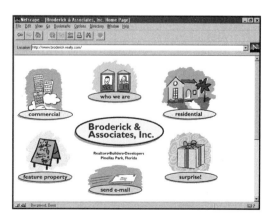

FIGURE 7-1

Broderick & Associates home page (http://www. broderick_realty.com/)

The best teacher seemed to be trial and error...change it, look at it, rechange it, look at it, and on and on...until I thought it was right. As cumbersome as it may seem, this is the best way to fine-tune the site. Trial and error taught me to streamline the time it took to change a Web page at home, send it to the server, and then view it. What used to take me hours to work over has now been condensed into minutes. And I've been approached by many other real estate companies in our area to lend a hand on their sites.

The biggest problem I kept facing was the ever-changing graphical interface of the Net. I would constantly be adjusting or changing the look and feel of the site because Netscape and Explorer and third party vendors kept enhancing the HTML language so they could include tables, marquees, video, etc. Script language now allows maps to embed links to other pages; the challenge is to create maps that are visually pleasing but compressed enough to view quickly. It's my impression that graphical designers and artists are enhancing sites for the better by creating visually dramatic pages, but this expertise comes with a price. These graphical interfaces are taking over the Net and squeezing the do-it-yourselfers out of the programming side of Web page creation.

I've tried to keep one axiom through all the technological changes the Web has seen over the past 18 months. I want a picture of the property, the information on the property, and where it is in relation to my small area of the world. I know from direct feedback, including an email message from a member of the House of Representatives, that many people enjoy the intuitive nature of our site, which allows the reader to easily navigate through the properties listed.

GETTING DIZZY?

Reading what Larry and Sean had to say may have left you a little dizzy, or simply more sure than ever that, like most agents, you are going to spend your time practicing real estate and leave Web page creation to someone else. That's fine. Knowing something about the process will make you a much wiser shopper.

If you want a bargain basement deal, you can get on the Web for as little as $100 a year, says Dr. Arnold Kling, founder of The Homebuyer's Fair, one of the first real estate-related sites on the Net. Arnold was a systems analyst for the Federal National Mortgage Association (FNMA) before he left to go into the Web business for himself.

Arnold warns that on the Web, as in real estate, you get what you pay for. Your hundred bucks is very unlikely to give you a page that displays the kind of graphics, links and information that will make potential homebuyers return to visit.

He estimates that a full-fledged Web site maintained by an outside contractor, with a constant inventory of approximately 12 listings, will cost about $5,000 a year. (If you do it yourself the cost drops like a rock—unless, of course, you calculate in your time.)

For an owner-broker to embark on a $5,000 investment in equipment and an additional $5,000 for advertising and promotion—a $10,000 gamble that promises to bring unknown structural changes in the way the business is run—is no small matter, especially given the favorable commission splits good agents have commanded since the 1980s. So it's no surprise that so many sites are indeed put up and maintained by individual agents themselves. Some of them—like Mario Giordani's—are among the best. That is no accident. Mario's whole previous career had prepared him to make the Web work for him when the time came.

GO SLOW

CONTACT

Arnold Kling
The Homebuyer's Fair
http://www.homefair.com
arnoldsk@us.net

Whatever your budget, the experts advise a slow immersion rather than a plunge. They tell you to set a budget for your Web venture just as you would for any other capital investment.

"You probably should spend no more than about 20 percent of your first-year Web budget up front," says Arnold Kling. "Save the rest for upgrades and publicity. However, do not make the mistake of putting up a half-done site and then doing all-out publicity. When Web pages say 'Under construction,' or 'Check back, we're adding more soon,' nobody ever comes back."

If you're dead set on having "a fully customized home page unlike any other," that's fine, but get ready to up that budget considerably, says Contour Software president Scott Cooley. "The custom route turns out to be the most complex and expensive way because it probably entails hiring programmers to write complex HTML programming routines. These kinds of interactive Web page projects can take many months to complete and the meter is ticking the whole time."

And then there's the really expensive option, operating your own Net server. To put up a totally independent page with your own hardware will entail a $15,000-plus investment because an Internet server (a high-end PC that does nothing but serve your Web pages up to those who connect to them) requires fast computers, dedicated phone lines, and someone to set them up and maintain them. ("The server is down" is the most dreaded statement on the Net. It means your site, for all intents and purposes, has ceased to exist.) Since most commercial service providers can offer all this to you for as little as $60 per month, investing in your own server is a questionable investment. For most agents doing so would be strictly a matter of vanity since they would also get their own domain name as well. In other words, if you use the local ISP SonicNet to serve up your Web pages, your address on the Internet might be something like *appleland-realty@sonic.net* and your Web page address would be *http://www.sonic.net/~appleland.html*.

Ah, but if Appleland Realty had its own server, it would also have its own domain name, and for email purposes broker Brad Jones would be *Brad@appleland.com*. The company's Web page address would be *http://www.appleland.com*. For some, this is the ultimate vanity license plate.

Only large operations that network their office computers truly benefit from operating their own servers. The vast majority of real estate operations will be best served by letting commercial Internet Service Providers handle this for them. Think of it as being a commercial tenant in someone else's building. When something goes wrong with the server, you don't have to fix it.

Hence, service providers have become the vehicle of choice for most companies simply because they are the most cost-effective alternative. Besides lower ongoing costs, putting your pages up on the ISP's servers reduces your initial investment substantially. That's the solution Scott Cooley recommends to his clients—an ISP, from design through maintenance. The costs are low, and growing competition will keep them low.

IF YOU DON'T HAVE THE TIME AND ENERGY...

Some service providers offer a turn-key solution that can have you up and running in a day or two. This is a quick and dirty job that won't win you any prizes for design or content. The providers use a boilerplate home page with the same standard categories of information for each subscribing company. You supply your company logo and data, and they have you up on the Web the next day. Some providers will do this for free; as part of their ISP contract with you they will offer so many megabytes of Web page space for you to use. Others charge a modest fee to put this trifle of a page up for you. But don't expect much. They are not going to put listings up for you or build a bunch of links to your favorite sites. This kind of Web page is the equivalent of mimeographed flyers stuffed under people's windshields in parking lots.

As the ISP marketplace has gotten increasingly crowded, some providers have gone "vertical," focusing on serving particular professions. Some ISPs serve doctors, others lawyers, and still others real estate agents. If you can find a local ISP that caters to agents, that may be your best bet. That ISP will not only understand your wishes better, but will also be providing a Web page of its own that lists and links all its real estate clients as well as the kind of local resources— like the chamber of commerce, schools, local weather information, etc.—that you would want included on your Web page. This saves you the time, space and trouble of building those links yourself.

Also, an ISP that specializes in providing service to real estate agents will undoubtedly offer variously priced plans that allow you to begin with a simple boilerplate page and slowly add predesigned listing pages as the need requires, at incremental cost.

Belonging to a local real estate-oriented ISP also increases your chances that out-of-town buyers will find you, because the Internet search engines will key in quickly on such a large local site if the buyer asks for "real estate AND San Francisco." HomeScout says the smallest site they key on has a hundred listings. Professional ISP groupings usually spawn interesting online discussion groups in which agents can swap tips and arrange deals among themselves.

PERSONAL ACCOUNT

Mary Kay Aufrance
Aufrance Associates
http://highsierra.com
tmaufr@highsierra.com

A Real Estate ISP?

If all this sounds good, but there is no local real estate-only ISP in your area, you might want to think about either starting one yourself (starting up an ISP is cheaper than you think) or encouraging an established ISP to start up a second one dedicated to agents.

Tom and Mary Kay Aufrance offers such services. Here's Mary Kay's sage advice on the subject:

> If you're thinking that there's probably more to the Internet than you have the time or inclination to master (and to keep up with), you are probably right. Plus, as the Internet matures as a marketing medium, there are other services beyond home pages, which only very skilled software developers can provide, such as searchable databases of properties for sale.
>
> Do-it-yourselfers can expect to find increasing avenues for getting involved in creating and maintaining their own presence on the Internet. That's because software developers like me are coming up with ways to involve you in the process and let you do things that are both useful and fun, such as update your own home page or property listings, upload photos to create home tours, or even have your own Web site. Think of all the control and fun that would offer: your own computer hooked up to the Internet,

so that you can put all kinds of information online for your business and your clients!

Our product, Real Estate Internet, offers the whole solution, if you are ready for it. Or we just let agents provide us with a business card, photos and listing flyers, and then stand back to let us take over.

However they first get a Web page, most real estate agents will want to make changes on it themselves. Some service providers will help you do that, others won't. Mary Kay has more to say on that:

> When pondering how much work you would like to put into your home page, or how to get your professional profile, photo and listings on the Internet, it helps to remember your goals and how much technical work you have the stomach for. However, it is a good idea to seek out services that will give you as much control over your pages as possible.

So, how do you get control without becoming a programmer? You'll have to seek out an Internet provider who does more than code up static home pages, which are time consuming and expensive. Although in these infant days of the commercial Internet many providers cannot offer special services that put you in control, it's a good idea to start looking for someone who can provide the features listed below:

- Online data entry forms. Not all services offer online data entry forms that you can use to enter your listings and photo files using your own Internet browser, such as America Online's Internet window or Netscape. This feature gives you more control over the content of your pages without having to learn all the technical intricacies of creating your pages. Plus, you should be able to go back to your data entry form whenever you want to change something, such as a listing price, a photo—or to include a special offer.

FIGURE 7-2

Aufrance – Sierra home page (http.//highsierra. com)

Our clients at Real Estate Internet love its online data entry feature for the control and immediacy it gives them. In fact, the agents have a lot of fun managing their own home pages and property listing pages, without having to know more than how to use their Web browser. Plus, having agents do their own data entry allows us as Internet providers to keep our costs lower, since we don't have to hire extra staff members to do things like change prices, correct misspellings or delete property listings that have sold.

- The ability to skip the online data entry. You should be able to merely send in your listing flyers or other information, if you get too busy or lose interest in doing it yourself.

- Your own Internet address, so that you can use this address as well as your email address on your business cards and print advertisements, to let everyone know where to find you on the Internet. Beware of services that bury your listings in some database, even if it is a searchable database. You need to have more than one way to be found.

- You need a "localized" and easy-to-find location. If a potential buyer is looking for real estate in Syracuse, what keywords do you think they will type into InfoSeek to find what they want? Most likely, they will key in "Syracuse Real Estate." Therefore, it's important that your listings or your home page be one of the Internet addresses that InfoSeek retrieves when this happens. If it's not, your Internet presence is not as visible as it could be. (However, as long as you have your own Internet address, you can register you own pages with the search engines. Go to *http://www.submit-it.com* and see how.)

- Find a reliable Internet provider, so that your pages will be available for view when someone tries to go there. If your potential clients get "DNS not found" when they click on a link to your page, you aren't getting your money's worth.

- Make sure there is more than one "road" leading to your home page. You should not be buried several clicks and pages down in the hierarchy of pages, or in a search database. In addition to getting your listings in a searchable database, which is fun for buyers who hunt for their dream home, the service you choose should give other ways for people to find you. For example, your agency should be listed in a page of hotlinks, or your personal home page should be on a list of local agents. This is because you want to increase the chances that you will be found by people who are clicking around out there in Cyberland, as they seek information about homes or real estate agents in your area.

- Get results! If your pages are not getting leads, try another service! In fact, we recommend that agents try both their national corporate service as well as our local service, to increase their chances of being found by prospective buyers and others who need their services. Your name should come up when a buyer makes a search for agents and offices in your local area. Your name also should come up when another agent located across the country wants to make a referral to a colleague out your way.

Of course, you could use your word processing software to create a home page and then ask some Internet provider to put it online. And it may even get you some calls. However, with many other agents getting exposure through searchable databases, clickable maps, extra links, and other ways to be found, your static age may decrease in effectiveness as the competition heats up and more real estate agents take advantage of the Internet.[3]

KEEP AN EYE ON IT

Whether or not you build your own Web page, look at it often once it's up. To get a slightly different perspective than Scott Cooley's Three Es (education, entertainment, and email) examine it from the perspective of Arnold Kling's three propositions:

- **An information proposition.** The information on your site has to be important and relevant to the customer.

    Think about what a relocating homebuyer would want: price ranges for the desired house size in different locations; school information; community information, including amenities and crime rates. Providing this type of data will help establish your credibility with the consumer.

    When you list homes on the Web, the consumer expects to see a photo. (One picture is still worth a thousand words.) Also, this is not a newspaper classified or MLS, so skip the obscure abbreviations and inside jargon. Take the time to describe the home in clear terms the consumer can understand.

- **A communication proposition.** Just putting up your phone number will not get you any business. You have to offer the consumer a reason to stay in touch with you, either by returning to your Web site or contacting you by email. Having a person merely "hit" your Web site without further contact is like having a homebuyer walk out of a property you are showing without even signing the register.

---

[3] *Used with permission from Aufrance Associates.*

Another variation on the communication proposition is to give the consumer a reason to revisit your Web site frequently. For example, if you keep an up-to-date list of homes recently sold in your area, active buyers and sellers will be motivated to come back and check often. Studies show that Web sites that draw repeat traffic are much more successful at generating business than sites the consumer visits only once.

- **A business proposition.** Explain what you can do for the homebuyer or home seller right *now* in such a way as to motivate the consumer to get a relationship started. For example, you might offer a free relocation kit to a potential out-of-town buyer.

  Your goal is to convert the surfer into a lead as soon as possible. One of the most common frustrations of businesses that market on the Web is to have thousands of hits without doing any business. While you cannot expect the consumer to select a real estate agent right away based on your Web site, you should offer something that gives the consumer an incentive to stay in contact with you. You can build the relationship from there.

Chapter 8 Links and Indexes: Use the Net to Build Response

Does a tree make a sound when it topples to earth if no one is around to hear it? You have to ask a similar question about Web pages: Does it matter whether you have a Web page if nobody can find it? Those real estate pages that get results for their owners are the ones that are publicized and share links with other real estate-related sites on the Web. Think of it as networking—on steroids.

▶ How Will They Find You?

▶ Working With a Publicist

▶ Ninety-five Percent Use the Search Engines

HOW WILL THEY FIND YOU?

Arnold Kling says getting professional help to publicize your Web site is probably worth more than you would think at first: "Web site publicity is an ongoing process. If you simply make one set of announcements and then stop, in six months your traffic will be way below its potential."

As with building a page in the first place, adding links to it from other sites is a process a do-it-yourselfer can accomplish. Building links from heavily traveled Web destinations is much like putting up a billboard on a busy street, only better. The billboard just tells potential customers who and where you are. A link does all that and brings the customer directly to you as well. The trick is getting busy sites to list you. Some make it easy; just fill out an onscreen form and it's done. Others make you cajole and bargain. But the time you spend building links will be well spent. Once he built his page, Rich Czeh probably spent more time than most establishing links to other sites:

> I started on the Net about six months ago. At first I just surfed and read. After deciding that this was the place to be, I purchased a program called "Web Page Construction Kit" with a software program and instruction book. It guaranteed you would have pages up in seven days. It worked; I was up in a week.
>
> After getting my page up I realized that I wouldn't get too many responses if people couldn't find me. So then I spent about a month finding places to put my links. It was a long and boring process, but I finally established 300-400 links and have managed to use only free links.
>
> I have found very little need to pay for being linked. So far I only have one link, the *Daily Reporter*, that I do pay for, and I did feel that one was worth it. It's really very hard to tell which ones work the best. Most people surf the Net, and by the time you talk to them they don't remember where they found you.

Rich says the most important links to have with other sites are: Infoseek, Yahoo, Alta Vista, Opentext, Webcrawler, Lycos, Magellan, and Who/Where, plus the Internet Yellow Pages, Internet Real Estate Directory, his local chamber of commerce, and the *Daily Reporter*, his local legal newspaper.

Rich says IRED (Internet Real Estate Directory) is his most important link to the Web marketplace as a whole, while his most important links to the local community are to the chamber of commerce and the *Daily Reporter*. He says Homebuyer's Fair is another important information source.

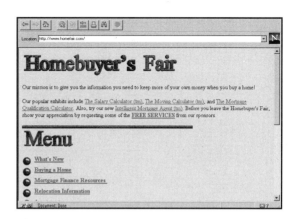

FIGURE 8-1

Homebuyer's Fair was one of the first mortgage pages on the Net (http://www. homefair.com/)

Arnold Kling's top link sites are Infoseek, Homebuyer's Fair Salary Calculator (which costs from $300 to $1,000 a year), IRED, Webcrawler ("Because AOL owns it, it gets tons of traffic"), Lycos, Prodigy's home page ("I think most people have to pay to get on, but our Salary Calculator has been listed for free some weeks, and we really get pounded when that happens"), Alta Vista, Excite, City.net, and Yahoo.

Most publicity techniques are not mysterious; getting the word out is getting the word out. To build traffic for RINtalk on the Realtor's Information Network, Webmaster Don Bodley posted this notice to subscribers on real estate forums:

```
Date: Sun, 18 Feb 96 13:34:13 EST
From: dbodleyx@reach.com (Donald E. Bodley )
To: skersnar@wco.com
Subject: RINtalk Update 2/17

+++++++++++++++++++++++
What's New on RINtalk?
Update for 2/17/96
+++++++++++++++++++++++

** The Webmaster's WWW Weekend Review reflects the
result of some random browsing over the past few
weeks. He has listed some of the more productive URLs
visited that can be of value to your personal and
business time online. Included is an Ultimate Search
Page for EXCITE and YAHOO, an Information Locators'
```

Reference page, and a listing of the 10 Biggest
Blunders that businesses make on the Web. You will
also find some excellent Marketing and Advertising
Sites with evaluations and related links. A veritable
gold mine of information to help in the construction
of a home page for your business or personal
presentations.

If (like Rich and Bill up in Alaska) you want to publicize your site
yourself, you have to assess whether the time commitment is worth
it. A good professional Web site publicist "probably can accomplish
more by using available free services than you could accomplish on
your own with paid advertising," says Kling.

Web publicists earn their keep by knowing how to build traffic to
a Web site by getting it listed in the right indexes with the right key
words. They can also be quite good at subtly planting information
about your site in key newsgroups and key listserv newsletters. I say
"subtly" because the Web culture takes offense at uninvited advertising and sales pitches. Such a message sent in a ham-handed way to
large numbers of people is called "spamming," and it is punished:
your email box will get "flamed"—that is, filled with angry email
from people who thought your sales pitch was offensive and intru-
sive. To avoid such penalties this kind of promotion is best left to
those who know their netiquette and can slide a mention of your site
naturally into their messages.

NEW LISTING SERVICE

Real estate agent and marketing specialist Greg White (*http://real-estate-
sales.com/*) commends the new listing services that take a buyer's requirements and data and search the Net for listings that match.

"I am all for services such as HomeScout and Matchpoint and have
many of my listings in both services," says Greg. "These services not
only give a URL to the listing, but also a URL to the home page on
which that listing appears. Both of these services provide only links
(they are stealing nothing.) They link a prospective buyer or seller to
your page. The more listings you have, the more traffic your page will
get as these services become more popular." Both Matchpoint and
HomeScout are supported by advertising.

FIGURE 8-2
Choice Realty's home page (http://real-estate-sales.com/)

WORKING WITH A PUBLICIST

Hiring a publicist doesn't relieve you of the responsibility to know what the publicist is doing for you. Before you sign on, ask questions and expect the same kind of periodic progress report you give sellers on your marketing efforts. Set up some kind of mechanism by which you can judge whether the publicist's efforts are paying off for you. If you have your own server, that's a simple enough matter. You can have a counter to track the number of visits your page gets. You can also monitor the level of email traffic your page generates. You might want to encourage email by offering to send inquirers a free map of the area or other incentive if they email you their address. As Larry Daniel told us, there are some responsibilities you don't relinquish.

Working with a professional publicist for a short initial period can be a tutorial experience that alerts you to strategies and techniques you can delegate to others for routine implementation.

PERSONAL ACCOUNT

Ray Dixon
WebEstate

http:/www1.mhv.net. webestate

webestate@mhv.net

Nothing Beats Tradition

WebEstate's Ray Dixon advises you to remember tried and true publicity as well:

Nothing beats traditional advertising methods. All the reciprocal links, search site entries, and even newsgroup and mailing list participation is great and generates visits. But, by all means, wherever you put your phone and fax numbers, put both your email and URL address as well. This in-

WebEstate

http://www1.mhv.net/~web estate

Provides participating agents with Internet broadcasting services, submitting their URLs to the most popular Web search engines, in addition to posting monthly broadcast messages to real estate newsgroups and mailing lists.

cludes, but is not limited to, your business cards, your phonebook display ads, newspaper display and classified ads, magazine ads, and even your business checks.

If you can convince a local newspaper editor to give you some coverage in the form of a review in their tech section or real estate section, all the better. Then, of course, there are radio and TV ads; if you do any of that, be sure to mention your Web site. All the big advertisers on TV do it now, both locally and nationally.

And if you haven't already, go to the WebEstate Global Real Estate Web and submit your free directory entry.

Ray says the most important alliance he has is with his clients through the Web Page Broker Package in which he offers wholesale rates for signing other agents up for WebEstate.

As we saw earlier, Ira and Carol Serkes give out free AOL and CompuServe disks at their open houses. On the disks they paste a sticker with their name, email and Web page addresses. You will see vendors doing the same thing at various trade shows. Both AOL and CompuServe offer free online hours to new users to get them started and will supply all the software disks you want to pass around. Since both services also offer Internet connections, this is a terrific, hassle-free way to get your customers connected to the Net.

And what a great way to build business! Since open houses rarely produce the buyer for the particular home you're holding open, the opportunity you seek there is to get new customers, customers who will feel enriched by their first contact with you. Visitors already connected to the Net will still ask about your page. A conversation with a fellow Net-head builds bonds on common ground—and brings a new visitor to your Web site.

Any way you look at it, Ira and Carol Serkes use the software gift to promote themselves as useful and helpful professionals. They promote their Web site as a place to visit and create a continuing link between themselves and their open house visitors and (more often than not) gain new customers. After all, who do you think will be the first ones to receive email from the grateful new AOL or CompuServe users?

NINETY-FIVE PERCENT USE THE SEARCH ENGINES

Mary Kay Aufrance says she agrees with a report in *PC World* magazine that 95 percent of Web users find what they are looking for with the search engines, so she spends a lot of time and energy making sure a search will lead to her REI customers:

CONTACT

Mary Kay Aufrance
Aufrance Associates
http://highsierra.com
tmaufr@highsierra.com

> I would search for the words "My-City Real Estate" and get links off all of the pages that come up in the top 20 any way I could…buy them or barter a link from my site to theirs. Pay particular attention to the words that give your pages a high score with the search engines. You should ideally show up on the first page of links, when someone searches for "Your-City Real Estate," and you can do this if you either include your keywords enough times in your text or in hidden comments on your HTML code.
>
> Start thinking about Internet providers (Web sites) the way you do magazines. There are many reasons to advertise with more than one. That includes your corporate site, if you belong to a big company. Lobby them to link out to any special home pages you have created elsewhere.

BAITING THE SEARCH ENGINES

If you have your own Internet address, you can register your own pages with the search engines. Barring that, as Mary Kay pointed out earlier, you have to make sure your Internet provider gets your page to come up when someone looks for real estate in your area. But Mary Kay says she and Tom aren't the only Tahoe providers who know how to put bait out for the search engines.

Just as you find AAAA Head Gasket Overhaulers in the front of the phone book, starting a Web page with A or a numeral will get you to the top of a list. One of Mary Kay's local competitors was loading up his page titles with every conceivable usage of the word "Tahoe." He had gotten so good at the trick that searches for anything with Tahoe in it put him in the hit list several times. What did she do about that? "I called him and asked him to change the titles!" (Right. And maybe he'll take his sign down while he's at it.) Actually, she says:

> I work hard to find out how the search engines do their indexing. Alta Vista seems to use only the contents of the <TITLE>, or at least it did. However, others look into the rest of the page. If you choose View Source on some of my pages (home page especially—also the non-real-estate clients like http://TahoeAccommodations.Com, you will see a lot of techniques that I use to capture the attention of search engine robots. I just make sure to get the keywords for a particular customer into the text as many times as I can. For example, if you search for "Lake Tahoe vacation," you will see my clients up high on the search list.
>
> Each engine's robot indexes the pages a little differently. And, knowing computer programmers, I am sure that some of the engines have extremely complex ways of deciding what to use to index the pages. For

Rossman & Mohring Appraisal Service
http://www.hway.net/ rossman/hints.htm
This service offers an excellent list of hints for submitting Web page URLs to make your page get better response.

example, some may ignore text that is in comments on pages; however, most seem to look at every word.

The one common denominator is that no search engine can index a page based on text found in graphics. Therefore, you can have a beautiful page with the coolest graphics and photography, yet it can be buried on the Internet because search engines won't find your keywords unless they are in text.

To find out where his business was coming from, Greg White actually took inventory of how and why people were accessing his Web page (*isell4u@accessone.com*). Then he (talk about Net angels!) posted complete visitor-by-visitor results on real estate listservs. Greg found that search engines brought him 17 visitors (8 from Yahoo, 5 from Alta Vista, 2 from Webcrawler, and 2 from Infoseek); 6 came from links to other pages, including loan sites; and 3 came from IRED. Real estate data compilers HomeScout and Matchpoint accounted for 1 each.

Chapter 9 Make a Web Site Business Plan

As this book went to press, many spectacular and otherwise excellent real estate Web sites were in the making but not yet up. When I asked a number of agents and other real estate professionals at conferences if they were planning to have Web sites, I discovered that many of them surfed the Net regularly, had developed a very sophisticated eye for good pages, and were well into the planning stage for their own sites—but hadn't created them yet. Obviously they took the planning phase very seriously.

As disappointing as it is not to be able to see their pages yet, those careful planners deserve honorable mention because whether you take five minutes or five months to do it, planning a page is a valuable step, and many of those professionals are bound to have successful Web sites.

This chapter takes up the most difficult (and rewarding) part of the process: figuring out exactly what you expect your Web site to do for you and say about you.

▶ A Business Plan Can Save Your Bacon

▶ You Yourself Enterprises

▶ It's Your Movie

▶ What You Get Out of It

A BUSINESS PLAN CAN
SAVE YOUR BACON

A real estate broker friend of mine is certain that he will never be bested by the owners of the other realty offices in his community because, he says, they all run their businesses "by accident" and he never does. He has a business plan that he consults and revises almost daily.

If you have ever owned a small business (one that actually survived and prospered) in a seasonal resort community, then you know something about business plans—whether or not you ever wrote one out. You don't survive without a clear strategy for balancing revenues to cope with the lean season. Having been a partner in such a business, I learned the value of knowing what we were going to do if Plan A didn't work.

As part of our plan we mapped out strategies to take advantage of our strong sense of the local community and how we could offer our product to as many people as possible. Because we had a plan that we believed in, when things didn't go well we didn't jettison our strategy and go running in panic after a better idea; instead we pressed harder to put our plan into action more efficiently and skillfully.

That notion—of knowing what you want to do and doing it better instead of chasing this way and that—is a useful one to keep in mind as you figure out how to make the Web work for you. Temptations and distractions are everywhere in the rapidly changing Internet environment. Certainties are few and far between. A good Web business plan can put some firmness into your sense of direction.

YOU YOURSELF
ENTERPRISES

If you're going to make (or remake) a Web page, you need to start with a very important question. Before we ask it, however, remember a key fact about you and your business. That fact is that *you* are a business. Whether the logo on your card says Century 21 or ABC Realty or Billy's Bigshot Buyers' Brokers, you are a one-person enterprise. The number on your shirt merely says you're in the race; you have to run that race, every day, all by yourself. What you run for is your commission checks, not for the greater glory and fatter bottom line of Main Street Realty.

Think of a Web site as a subsidiary of that one-person enterprise. Your Web page will be like an outpost or interactive branch office of your business, a fully owned subsidiary of "You Yourself Real Estate Enterprises" (which currently may happen to be affiliated with Main Street Realty or Coldwell Banker or RE/MAX). Your Web site is (or should be) an electronic delivery van, a kiosk, a virtual advertising agency, an ever-hospitable concierge, working 24 hours a day for you.

As we saw, Mario Giordani runs his Home Port site as a fully functioning subsidiary with many enterprises buzzing along at one time, all focused on one thing: to keep Mario at the top of the charts for sales in his area. You can be sure that Mario uses and has used all the other media; you can be sure he would drop his Web site like a hot rock if it didn't pull business for him. But it does. Most of his business leads, inquiries and referrals now come from email and his Web site.

Similarly, Alice Held was a successful agent long before the Web came along; if her page didn't pull for her and enhance her finesse at practicing real estate, she'd discard it. Alice says any real estate agent can do what she has done with her Web page. The secret, she says, is to "create and develop a niche for yourself and make your Web site fit that."

Sounds simple, but to play catch-up with agents like Alice and Mario does not merely mean you pick up the phone and yell, "Get me a Web site like Alice's, and get it here fast!" You can't just order a good Web site the way you order a platter of cold cuts from the deli.

HERE COMES THE QUESTION

Before ordering or constructing your page, ask yourself the following question:

"What's the point?"

What's the destination? What's the goal? You Yourself Realty Enterprises can only be a reflection of something, an extension of something. You have to say what that "something" is. What's the point? What do you want people to know and remember about you?

HI, I'M NOT HOME, BUT COME ON IN!

Whether or not you want it so, your Web page will be a picture of you and what you have to offer buyers and sellers. Think of your home page as a house that's never locked. People are invited to walk right in (or climb in through the window if they want to), go through your dresser drawers and closets, peruse your bookshelves, grab an apple out of the refrigerator, and depart any time they want to—with or without leaving you a note saying they came to visit. So, what impression of you do you want your Web visitors to carry away with them?

THE PEOPLE YOU DRAW TO YOURSELF

The old sales motto has it that "there's a fanny for every seat." You hear agents mutter that little reminder to themselves as they preview some OPT (overpriced turkey) of a listing with a sinkful of dishes and a basement full of dry rot. "At the right price, someone will buy this place," they remind themselves, "and I guess I don't mind being the one who sells it."

Some people love selling places like that. They're at home with Title I and 203k financing, they love to talk about French drains, seismic retrofits, house jacks, and tearing out kitchens; they have a stable of "fixer-upper" buyers who come running whenever they hear that another wreck with a leaning chimney has just hit the market. Agents who work well with such listings view every remodeled junker as a patient saved.

Other agents don't. New houses on brand new streets, the smell of fresh concrete and drying paint, those little sapling trees in front held up with stakes and guywires, helping people choose between two kinds of bathroom vanities and three options for the kitchen countertops, making sure the options and extras buyers pick fit under the ceiling of the purchase loan. Now you're talking, some agents say. That's where I know my stuff and shine like the beautiful crystal chandelier my subdivision contractor offers as a deluxe option in the full dining room.

WOULD YOU DO THIS?

It's not just the kind of real estate you like to sell that determines what kind of customers you will tend to draw with your Web site. Other kinds of choices you make will definitely tend to attract "your" kind of people and send others surfing on their way. For example, would you post a notice like this at your Web site?

Frames ALERT!

This document is designed to be viewed using Netscape 2.0's Frame features.

If you are seeing this message, you are using a frame-challenged browser.

A frame-capable browser can be obtained from Netscape Communications.

I personally would not post a notice in language that blatant. It seems to me that if you adopt a new HTML option like frames, you need to make sure that people with a "frame-challenged browser" can either upgrade their browser directly from your site (by your providing a link to a site where the upgrade can be downloaded) or that the page will display in some acceptable way for most browsers.

I think it's the page owner's responsibility to make a page inviting and accessible. But whether or not *you* would post a warning to the frame-challenged or pick a blue sky background for your home page or include a custom page on local hotels are choices that will lead potential customers toward you or away from you as those choices add up to a picture of who you are and how you operate.

What kind of agent are you? What niche can you build for yourself so that you will stand out? How can a Web page be put together to draw the people you deal with best? How much money do you have to budget to make sure your Web investment pays off? Are the costs of developing your Web site an expense item or should they be capitalized and depreciated over time? How long are you prepared to wait before getting business from your Web investment? And what yardstick are you going to use to measure its success? How do you work your Web page into the flow of your other business goals and activities?

These questions should be familiar. The promotional, time-management and motivational tapes, books, seminars, techniques, bumperstickers and resolutions you invest in your regular real estate practice also apply to building and using a Web page. The difference is that building a Web page is not like signing a contract for magazine advertising or buying a new fax/scanner/answering machine or taking a seminar on listing techniques or hanging your license with a new real estate office. Done properly, building a Web site can be a much bigger move than all those things put together.

IT'S YOUR MOVIE

We refined the question "What's the point?" into another one: "What do I want?" Now, if the point is to get business for you by promoting your business with a Web site, we have to refine the question again: "What am I good at?" Vanity may be a sin, but when it comes to promotion, being overly modest is a much deadlier sin. Think of your Web page as a movie; are you willing to star in it? If you don't star, who—or what—will? If you are in Hawaii or Florida, a beach could be your star, as long as you build your Web site in a way that will make people pick you to help them buy their own stretch of beach. Inevitably, the focus will be on you at some point.

Everyone, it has been said, is a star in the movie that makes up their life. The only stories we really can tell are our own. Movie producers want to hear ideas for screenplays pitched in a single sentence called a high concept. What's yours? "Camera-Toting Real Estate Agent Brings You Alaska" is a marketing high concept we've already talked about for Bill Hutchinson. "The Agent with the Palace Listed in Thailand" is one memorable image of Alice Held.

Remember that your Web page is like a poster asking people to come see your movie. You want it to be inviting. "Eager-Looking Gentleman Says He's a Professional CRS and GRI." What a snooze! "Honest Young Woman Offers to Work Really Hard for Buyers in Delaware." The storyline seems a little fuzzy.

Asking yourself what is the focus of your enterprise is another way of phrasing the previous question. Experts often say the most important element in marketing is focus. What is the specialty niche or area of growing reputation you are carving out for yourself? If you are a CRS and a GRI, how do you step out and say those designations add up to something homeseekers will want to know more about? How do you differentiate yourself from the herd?

HONOR YOUR OWN FOOTSTEPS

One top producer I know markets herself with a question: "Who do other agents come to when they have a question about real estate?" Now, that's bold. It works for her because other agents—from her own and other offices—actually do come to her with their real estate questions. Even people who might resent her for saying so have to admit it's true.

Use your Web page to play to your strengths. If you like doing something it will be easier to convince others that you are good at it. What you've done well and happily in the past, and perhaps taken for granted, is a clue to what you can do next without driving yourself crazy. First-time buyers, ranch properties, 1031 exchanges, REOs, disaster-damaged properties, special techniques needed to market log cabins, busy buyers who want you to anticipate and take care of their needs…specialize in familiar territory.

WHAT YOU GET OUT OF IT

As you address all those questions, it may be helpful to divide Web page benefits into three categories: tangible benefits, expected benefits, and indulgences.

- **Tangible benefits** are the minimal rewards you get, such as added exposure and email responses from buyers and sellers.

- **Expected benefits** are those you anticipate receiving if you do everything right and have a little patience. This certainly includes an increase in sales and listings. How much of an increase depends on your expectations.

- **Indulgences** are those motives you have to admit to yourself if to no one else. For example, if your page meets none of your expectations, but you still want it up, then something else is at work here: ego. Admit it, you like having a Web page. You like having your picture on the Web. You like having that URL and email address on your cards and stationary. There's nothing wrong with any of those reasons.

Any one of these three, or any combination of them is reason enough to justify your Web project. It's only important that you understand *why* you're doing it, because that will determine *how* you do it.

TARGET MARKET WORKSHEET

There are plenty of books out to tell you how to create business plans, and the Web itself offers a wide variety of marketing resources. But in order to verify that there's a need for the services you want to provide before you propose to fill them, you might take an opportunity to jot down some questions and answers about your intended market:

1. **Who are your intended customers?**

2. **What do they need (want)?**

3. **How can you fill those needs?**

4. **What do you uniquely have to offer them?**

FURTHER WEB-SPECIFIC STEPS TO REMEMBER:

- Surf the Web every day. Check out other real estate sites and analyze how they work.

- Keep your surfing bookmarks organized in some way so that you can return to sites you liked to see how their owners are changing them over time. (Back up your bookmarks so you don't lose them.)

- Make a habit of developing URL trading partners who tip you off on sites that fit your business plan. Do the same for them.

- Visit Downtown Anywhere (*http://www.vmedia.com/books/ira/data/sect103/list1.htm*) to keep tabs on some of your slick competition for the attentions of the Web shopper.

- Check out listserv forums and newsgroups; join at least one related to your specialty or focus.

- Create signature files for your email to reinforce your message.

- Make regular product/service announcements and bulletins to post in bulletin boards and discussion groups.

- Refine your bulletins into press releases and distribute them to the media. Develop a press packet/brochure to hand out in case you are interviewed or asked to participate on a convention panel or radio/TV discussion.

- If the very idea of being asked some day to appear on a panel as an expert in your professional specialty seems absurd to you, then go back and rework your high concept until you start believing you're up to something worth talking about.

Chapter *10* Birds of a Feather: MLS, Organizations, VANs, and Alliances

In Chapter 9 we talked about using the Web to put yourself in control of your own real estate destiny. Although later in this chapter we'll discuss Web developments likely to support and enhance the role of both listing and selling agents, other powerful developments bound to affect your career are harder to measure. Let's take a look at some.

- ▶ Wrestling for Position
- ▶ Winning Strategies Shaping Up
- ▶ Four Elements of Success
- ▶ The Missing Link

WRESTLING FOR POSITION

When you hear news about Coldwell Banker, C-21 and ERA becoming part of a giant conglomerate, AT&T offering its Internet customers discounted access to CompuServe, or NAR negotiating a far-ranging strategic agreement, how does all that affect you? The changes involving the Internet and the real estate business are dizzying and the outcomes utterly uncertain.

Competition for effective placement on the Web is fierce. Like homesteaders racing across the plains to stake out prime land before someone beats them to it, a host of Web services and vendors are vying for your loyalty and those of your buyers and sellers.

Positioning your Web pages for maximum effectiveness becomes tricky when you factor in all the forces driving the real estate market. How do you take advantage of trends? What strategic alliances do you need to make in order to prosper? How are you affected by MLS mergers in your area? Who will be the industry's winners and losers?

Clearly we are seeing MLS databanks opening themselves up on the Web. And we are seeing services like Matchpoint, HomeScout and BRE giving homebuyers easy ways to reach actual property listings and useful information, unimpeded by the need to surf through online agent resumes and group photos of Broker Bob and the gang at We're Still Here Realty. If there is any rule of thumb for success on the Web, it seems to be, as we said earlier, that those who provide prospective customers with open access and a good reason to come back prevail over competitors who don't.

WHAT'S MINE IS MINE, WHAT'S YOURS IS OURS

"Whoever controls the listings controls the real estate market." Remember the old days (a year or two ago) when you could say something like that with a straight face and everyone within listening distance would nod in agreement? No longer. Can agents and offices "own" listings once sellers believe they have genuine alternatives to the traditional MLS process? The coming of the Internet has made it harder to answer that question with a simple yes or no.

In the controversy over proprietary control of listing information, the Internet has so far been a Pandora's box. When a listing service brags of its effectiveness because buyers are accessing it and going to real estate offices bearing printouts of listings they want to see, can it then hold those buyers guilty of copyright infringement? Some attorneys say so. Others suggest that providing that very ease of access is an act of diligence on behalf of the seller. They say failure to provide such access could be construed as a breech of an agent's fiduciary duty. The whole copyright question on the Net is a gray area.

In any event, say others, Web sites that attempt to put limits on sharing information will erect gates and barriers that keep their Web pages from getting visitors. They say that if the battle to do business is viewed as a battle to control information, it is a battle lost in advance because no one controls information on the Internet. Check out Rogue Web (*http://www.rogueweb.com/*) to sample more of that view.

When the National Association of Realtors unveiled RIN, the Realtors Information Network, at the 1995 NAR convention in Atlanta, the California Association of Realtors quickly followed with its California Living Network tied to a national version, Living Network USA, that quickly gave RIN a run for its money by aggressively opening the public's access to information.

FOR SALE BY OWNER

Some say the real estate establishment—including big companies that practice dual agency and view their listings as their lifeblood—is missing the mark in using the Internet. Some say that within the next decade listing a home for sale on the Internet will be as easy and commonplace as listing a phone number. FSBOs will be the norm rather than the exception, dual agency will go out the window, and the vast majority of agents will represent buyers exclusively.

Certainly the openness of the Net encourages offering homes for sale by owner, and there is no shortage of Web resources for those who want to take a stab at saving themselves a real estate commission.

"For millions of people buying or selling property on their own, the job just got easier," said the announcement when By Owner Online (*http://www.by-owner-ol.com*) introduced its Web site. "Through this one-stop service, buyers and sellers use a simple point-and-click process to view everything from single family homes, condominiums, and manufactured homes, to vacant land, commercial property, vacation rentals, and timeshare."

Vermont By Owner Magazine (*http://www.wegrew.com/*) was launched as a Net sideline by an active agent, Elizabeth Wilkel, who saw a deeply entrenched taste in her state for by-owner sales and stepped up to capitalize on it rather than watching from the sidelines while someone else did it instead. She says her real estate brokerage is prospering right along with her publishing venture.. But some real estate agents are very sure, as one puts it, that "once that FSBO database is in place as competition, we will all learn what 'brokering' is worth in a tech-based free marketplace, and it sure won't be six to seven percent!"

Many say the Internet is poised to turn the real estate market on its ear, casting out some traditional players and exalting others who haven't even weighed in yet. Seaborn "Steve" Wicker, a principal in TEN31 Investments, Inc., sees Web-savvy investors and even home buyers quickly surpassing agents in real estate sophistication:

CONTACT

Steve Wicker
http://www.1031.com
seaborn@Ten31.com

> With today's technology and especially the Internet, a knowledgeable person could complete transactions anywhere. Salespeople are no competition at all to the prepared person. Almost any real estate agent could be used as a "free taxi driver" to take people to see property and chauffeur them various places. However, tomorrow's real estate investors will be able to place their property on the market and pick out property without an agent. They will be able to do it on their home televisions. What they will need is what I call "transaction engineers" to prepare the best possible agreement with terms, mortgages, negotiations, etc. The day of the dual agent is already over. Some of them just do not know it yet! It is like the obituary of John Averageman: he was born in 1965, died in 1983, and buried in 1996; he just wouldn't fall over!

Steve says real estate's ranks will continue to shrink the way the ranks of the mortgage lending industry have thinned: "Agents left the business by the thousands in the 1980s, and will continue to do so unless they adapt." He goes so far as to say that the average real estate company will disappear, driven out of business by the laptop and the television.

NOT SO FAST

Observers don't all share those apocalyptic views. Ina Bechhoefer, editor of the *Guide to Real Estate and Mortgage Banking Software*, gives three broad reasons why the young bulls offering to throw out the old real estate order will have to wait their turn. For one thing, the World Wide Web market is largely confined at this point to the younger, well-educated segment of the buying populace. The Web so far lacks the clout, penetration and established reliability to dictate how the larger real estate market will fare. Second, she points out that FSBO-based systems of various sorts have waxed and waned over the years—waxing in active markets and waning under tight money conditions when sellers need all the expert help they can get to find buyers. There are various indications that the red hot real estate markets of recent decades will be rarer, briefer and more localized from now on. Finally, Ina says, it is naive to underestimate the power of the

CONTACT

Don West
Omni Realty of Virginia
http://www.estatenet.com/
agents/omni/agent.htm

CONTACT

Tim Cowles
The RE Place
http://www.replace.com

CONTACT

Susan Packer
Frank Howard
Allen/Hernandez Realty
Panther48@aol.com

NAR and the large real estate franchises: "Their hold on the market in certain parts of the country is impossible to break."

Don West adds that "forecasters of the demise of the listing agents have an ax to grind, usually their own. Maybe building their own rice bowl." Though Don says he is perfectly willing to help FSBO's sell their homes, "Daily I see buyers who are afraid of dealing with 'for sale by owners.' Why? They do not trust the other principal."

Idaho real estate consultant Tim Cowles suggests that the more closely listing agents observe the way relocating buyers actually use the Web, the more secure they can feel about their role in the process:

> Has anyone thought through the buyer process from a buyer's viewpoint? All the email off the 200 home pages I manage have asked for relocation information and have yet to ask for information about a specific home. Buyers look at listings to see what's out there. When they get serious, they contact an agent. Would you move anywhere and buy without local advice and knowledge? Unlikely.

California agent Susan Packer says real estate transactions are simply too complicated for most sellers to handle on their own:

> An agent's role has actually increased as the technology has increased. When I started selling real estate twenty years ago, we had one-page contracts and no disclosures. Now we have six pages of contract and four pages of seller's disclosure statements in addition to disclosures for agency, hazardous materials, earthquakes, lead paint, etc. The role of an agent is to explain and interpret this information for the client. The idea that we would become unnecessary because people can browse listings on the Internet would assume that agents function as tour guides and nothing more. In reality that is the smallest portion of our job.

Though good agents may continue to thrive, most observers say brick-and-mortar real estate offices will—like bank branches—grow fewer and farther between. Certainly, with so many entrenched players and some well-bankrolled and technology-rich contenders weighing in to do Web real estate on a national scale, the next few years are bound to litter the information superhighway with some hefty-looking bones. And let's not forget that some of the major players aren't even on the Web yet.

WINNING STRATEGIES SHAPING UP

The big national real estate companies were among the first to recognize the potential of the Web to enhance the reach of their networks of offices and affiliates. Companies like Century 21, RE/MAX and Coldwell Banker recognized the opportunity to stake out a broader electronic presence for themselves and jumped onto the Web early.

The large real estate companies can leverage their strengths very effectively on the Web when they want to. Coldwell Banker (*http://www.coldwellbanker.com/*) caters to a broad range of interests with its Web site. It offers good relocation information, including a comparison of home prices in various cities, and extensive consumer tips. For example, there's a page devoted to information on home inspections and warranties. For homeowners and agents alike, the Coldwell Banker site offers a disclosure treasure-trove; the section on earthquakes is remarkably authoritative and well crafted.

When NETCOM reached a strategic agreement with Netscape Communications to offer NETCOM subscribers an enhance browser, Coldwell Banker, which recently became a corporate sibling to Century 21 and ERA, was one of the first affinity contractors to sign on to bring real estate agents and consumers to the Internet utilizing the NETCOM-Netscape relationship.

CONTACT

Gary Edwards
Property Transaction Network
ge@ptn.xo.com

Gary Edwards and his associates with the Property Transaction Network have been developing a beta version of their system for RE/MAX of California that will employ videoconferencing and electronic networking to link all participants in a real estate transaction. The second stage of the rollout involves 45 offices. Next, the system will be marketed to other major franchises.

Century 21 uses its AOL presence as a de facto wide-area network for its affiliated offices and agents. Eager to capture as much of the relocation and referral dollar as they can, the franchises are forging self-enclosed webs within the Web.

CAR'S LIVING NETWORK

The California Association of Realtors' California Living Network Web site(*http://ca.living.net*), launched in November 1995, is one of the largest sources for California property listings on the Web. As this book went to press, CAR had listings in all but one California county and expected to have 90 percent of active California home listings on the California Living Network by summer, 1996.

ListingLink, a Santa Monica, California-based Internet publishing company, works with CAR, the nation's largest state association of realtors, to operate Living Network USA and the California Living Network. Property listings are uploaded to the Web sites from several sources, including individual agents and brokerage companies, regional multiple listing services, and national foreclosure databases maintained by Fannie Mae and Freddie Mac. Included are demographic, school, economic, and travel/leisure information about specific communities.

REAL ESTATE SEARCH ENGINES

Ninety-five percent of Net shoppers, we noted earlier, use search engines as the quickest way to find what they're seeking. The newest entrants to the competition to shape the Web real estate market are betting that buyer insistence on simple, direct access to product information will continue to carry the day.

Matchpoint calls itself "the simplest way to look at homes advertised on the World Wide Web." A buyer fills out a customer search template, and "you only enter your requirements once" unless you want to change your requirements. Matchpoint then brings up a list of homes matching the buyer's requirements and lets buyers click on the particular homes they want to see. The buyers are then taken to a Web page where the home is described in detail.

Matchpoint doesn't search databases; agents sign on to link their listings to it. Matchpoint notifies prospective buyers of new listings and changed listings by matching all prospective buyers' search templates with new listings and changed listings every 24 hours. When matches occur, the buyer is notified automatically by email to dial up the home listing in the broker's site.

The Cobalt Group's equivalent is called HomeScout, which works with multiple real estate Web site databases to provide users with summary information on more than 200,000 homes. HomeScout works much like Internet search engines such as Webcrawler and InfoSeek, searching real estate agency and real estate service Web sites for homes matching buyer criteria.

Buyer's Resource East (Buyer's Resource is a national exclusive buyer agency franchise system) is just beginning to pick up momentum. The company is in the process of forging an agreement to interface with the MARS electronic mortgage system to provide mortgage financing nationwide under the aegis of a "superbroker" licensed in all 50 states.

Participating buyer's brokers and any number of participating lenders agree to exchange mortgage information via computer. Buyer's Resource/MARS will use computerized loan origination to take applications in participating buyer broker offices.

A key component in the BRE business plan is creating a national for-sale-by-owner network (*www.fisbos.com*). Linda Rousseau, BRE's project manager, says that within six months the company expects to add 300–500 properties a week, with broker loading by participating realties.

BRE takes the most aggressive posture toward reshaping organized real estate, claiming that "the base lead procurement and MLS listing system…is coming to the end of its useful life," to be replaced, BRE says, by computer-based consumer-friendly systems with place for listing brokers in the equation.

FOUR ELEMENTS OF SUCCESS

When Visual Listings of Brea, California, added the Desert Area Multiple Listings Service to its Homeseekers Internet Web site (*http://www.homeseekers.com*) in February, 1996, those 6,000 additional listings brought Homeseekers' total number of listings available for Southern California to just under 50,000 properties.

Visual Listings president John Giaimo says that adding all the California desert resort cities to the listings for the Greater Inland Valleys MLS, the Southern California MLS (including all of Orange County and portions of Los Angeles and Long Beach) and the Greater South Bay Regional MLS brought Homeseekers enough critical mass in

FIGURE 10-1
Homeseekers' Web site carries listings of over 50,000 southern California properties (http://www. homeseekers.com/)

those communities that "we are receiving over 30,000 accesses a day." He says brokers are now talking about clients entering their offices with printouts of the selected homes in hand.

Information provided from the participating MLS services is updated every business day from actual MLS databases. The Visual Listings search engine is "extremely powerful," says Giaimo, with 50 searchable ways of finding selected homes in about five seconds.

Unlike some rival services, Homeseekers offers its base service (a listing with photo and description, including office and agent names and phone numbers) for free. Costs are now partly defrayed by advertising, with sponsors such as Stewart Title, Centerpoint Mortgage and Orange Coast Title signing on not only as advertisers, but as potential participants in what can become a functioning value-added network (VAN). That is where experts see the World Wide Web heading as a real estate marketplace, with links to a mortgage calculator, mortgage lenders, escrow companies, real estate attorneys, mapping services, and the full range of service providers contributing to a transaction.

Giaimo says the initial Homeseekers business plan called for advertisers to provide 40 percent of revenues, with the remainder coming from creating and servicing Web pages for individual agents. Agents can have their home page on the system for $50 a year, linked to all their MLS listings. Listings are updated every day, a service that competitors to MLS-linked services cannot match. Sponsors like Stewart Title are drawn to that kind of stability.

A small multiple listing service in central Oregon with much less powerful hardware missed by two weeks beating Homeseekers for the honor of starting this revolutionary trend toward making MLS listings available on the Web at no cost to member agents.

Working in conjunction with Computer Software Systems (CSS) of Bend, Oregon, the MLS of Central Oregon put the entire Central Oregon residential MLS listing on the Web (*http://bendor.com/real_estate/*) to offer buyers the opportunity to preview photos and descriptions of 2,600 Oregon houses for sale, without an agent looking over their shoulders.

Gary Mart, president of CSS, observes, "The Internet version of the listing has another huge advantage over the MLS book. The viewer can have the system automatically select just the houses that meet their criteria prior to meeting with their agent."

"As awareness of this service has grown," says Gary, "we've been growing at 50 percent per month." He says individual real estate agents are now signing up for their own Web pages.

Moore Data Management Services, headquartered in Toronto, has made the Chicago-based Multiple Listing Service of Northern Illinois—the largest MLS in North America—first to go on the Net via a new service called CyberHomes (*http://www.cyberhomes.com*).

At this writing, Moore had agreements with multiple listing services in several other states and provinces in North America representing more than 150,000 listings now going online, including MLS groups in California, Pennsylvania, New York, Texas, Colorado, Arkansas, Washington, Arizona, and Nova Scotia.

Using map data provided by ETAK of Menlo Park, California, CyberHomes' mapping application lets visitors select homes by price, by criteria such as number of bedrooms and baths, and by specific location. Homes selected for review can be plotted on an easy-to-read map of the area. Web visitors can zoom in on a particular map location and ask for listings radiating out from the selected spot.

Do companies like Homeseekers, Computer Software Systems and CyberHomes hold the keys to the real estate marketing revolution? Some observers say they have carved out a big piece of it by:

- Allying themselves with MLS services rather than competing with them.

- Giving member agents' listings initial free access to the Web marketplace so as to add value to MLS membership rather than undermining it.

- Offering agents voluntary access to further services like Web page creation (at additional cost, adding to sustaining revenues).

- Giving service providers a clear incentive to advertise in this new marketing venue and thereby position themselves to offer value-added services (mortgage, title, inspection, insurance, etc.) as these Web marketplace sites evolve into inexpensive, fully functioning value-added networks.

PERSONAL ACCOUNT

Mac Partlow
Joint Marketing Solutions
MR.MAC@pobox.com

Consumer Power

Real estate consultant Mac Partlow of Joint Marketing Solutions in Laguna Niguel, California, says individual consumers and agents will gain power from the coming of the Web:

> From my perspective, the first identifiable winners from the changes in real estate taking place on the Internet and the World Wide Web will be individual consumers. Easy access to MLS information from visionary services such as Homeseekers and CAR's California Living Network will allow consumers to make selections of homes prior to calling an agent. The consumer will be

better informed and prepared for what's available in the market when they finally call an agent.

The existing industry players who will emerge as winners are more difficult to identify. MLS organizations and their traditional vendors will be under continuous pressure to meet the demands of the public for access to formerly proprietary information. Those who assume a protective posture will not survive, in my opinion.

Also, as more and more individual agents put their own personal home pages on the Web, get their own email addresses, get wired to the Web from their home, they will begin to receive calls, leads, and business *directly*, without the traditional filter of the brokerage house advertising and referral program, etc. When this begins to occur on a regular basis, many agents will begin to ask themselves, "Why do I need this broker?" So real estate offices could be big losers if the Internet and World Wide Web become as powerful as some are predicting.

The Web, as we've seen, does offer individual agents extraordinary opportunities to leverage their reach. But the big real estate franchises didn't get that way by ignoring market realities. If their first efforts to harness the Web represented a reconnaissance in force, their subsequent efforts will be to adapt where they cannot dictate. Look to the corporate giants to set the pace, for example, in offering sophisticated Web training and marketing tools for agents.

THE MISSING LINK

CONTACT

Jody Lane
TitleLink
http://www.computek.net/ public/fermier/

jlane@titlink.com

In spring 1996, TitleLink arrived on the Internet offering to leverage the World Wide Web into a widely affordable and fully functioning real estate and mortgage lending marketplace. If TitleLink and systems like it are widely adopted, says Ina Bechhoefer, that development will represent a major functional enhancement for real estate on the Web.

Gary Edwards calls TitleLink the most crucial component in the development of his Property Transaction Network. TitleLink is an online order, communication and tracking system for escrow and title services. Its Internet version of a Lotus Notes-based system connects title insurance and settlement providers to all the professionals participating in a real estate or mortgage loan closing.

A special attraction for budget-conscious small offices and individual agents is that TitleLink's Internet version does not require you to use Lotus Notes to access and use this "electronic closing table."

"By using the Net, we can offer a lower price and easier accessibility. There's no software to install," says TitleLink president Jody Lane. "What we've done is speed up the escrow process and find a way to involve individual real estate agents we didn't have before."

For a flat fee of $28.50 a month, TitleLink allows users large and small to connect (through pass codes) to a secure Web site and see all correspondence, documents, and requests on each of their transactions. They can see exactly what the title company has done on their specific transactions and know when it was done.

REAL ESTATE AGENTS BECOME MORE VALUABLE

Services like TitleLink permit individual real estate agents to communicate with the title company, lender, appraiser, attorney, and other brokers within their own secure database. "This allows the real estate agent to offer customer service that before was impossible," Jody says. "At present the only way we are going to allow the seller or buyer to access the system is through a real estate agent. Otherwise we nullify the efficiencies the system produces because we have to conduct the whole orchestra at the pace of the slowest and least proficient players, the principals."

Principals will only see information or documents sent to them. But buyers' and sellers' questions about the status of the transaction will be answered much more quickly, clearly, and accurately.

A demo of the process from the initial order to final closing is available at TitleLink's Web site (*http://www.titlelink.com/*).

As this book went to print, TitleLink was about to offer add-on messaging capabilities. "Let's say the lender, Countrywide, has sent loan documents to an office of Fidelity Title. With this service the computer will immediately generate a phone call, 'Closing documents were just sent to you,' referencing what was sent," Jody explains.

With this added service, real estate and mortgage brokers can have these same computer-generated calls sent to buyers, sellers and borrowers—and will be able to access the TitleLink database from their phones when they're out in the field. Says Jody, "That makes real estate agents better, more professional and, in turn, more valuable to their customers."

As mentioned earlier, CAR and Homeseekers both have chosen more established rival Data Track Systems (*http://www.datatrac.com*). In March 1996, Data Track formed a strategic partnership with Contour Software. Contour will package Data Track software solutions with Internet access in the Contour suite of products.

FIGURE 10-2
Data Track Sys-tem's home page (http://www. datatrac.com/)

Russ Bergeron, general manager of Southern California Multiple Listing Service and a partner in Homeseekers, says, "We have been searching for a method to link all of the participants in a real estate transaction in order to speed up the closing process. Data Track has developed Internet solutions that can do just that."

II Commercial Real Estate, REITs, 1031s, and Lenders

One way to get a deeper sense of how the Web is likely to affect your business is to take a look at the way it affects colleagues you deal with less frequently, such as lenders and commercial brokers. If real estate agents can expect to face downward pressure on their commissions, it's instructive to see how lenders like Dick Lepre use the Web to make more money by charging less. To find out what the Internet can offer as a real estate company's "intranet" or internal network, it's helpful to learn about a real estate trust (Kranzco REIT in Pennsylvania) enjoying that cost-saving synergy right now.

▶ Technology Is Key for Commercial Real Estate

▶ Setting Up Networks

▶ Real Estate Investment Trusts

▶ Net Lenders

TECHNOLOGY IS KEY FOR COMMERCIAL REAL ESTATE

Some will tell you the Internet was made for commercial real estate, even though residential agents are ahead of their commercial colleagues in recognizing the marketing potential of the Internet.

Others say the Internet will be good for some—but not many—commercial brokers, with technology determining who survives. "We're still in the dinosaur age for many brokers," says CCIM Greg Laycock, who predicts that the winnowing out over the next five years will be enormous, with a current pool of around 80,000 active commercial real estate agents being thinned down within five years to some 6,000 technologically sophisticated (and very prosperous) practitioners. He says many commercial brokers who ignored the technological revolution are now "too afraid of losing control of their time" to face getting the training necessary to alter their business practices and catch up.

John M. "Jack" Peckham III, CCIM—Boston-based author of *Master Guide to Income Property Brokerage*, the bible of commercial real estate practice, and a leading expert and speaker on the Web as a commercial real estate cybermarket—doesn't see the thinning out of commercial practitioners by technology as being that drastic, but agrees that the commercial ranks will shrink by at least a third over the next decade.

T. J. Anderson is one longtime commercial specialist who believes the Web will one day soon provide a transparent, coherent marketplace used by all active commercial brokers. Her current project is putting together an international commercial forum.

T. J. has two Web sites, the Austin Real Estate Connection (*http://www.austinre.com*) and Internet Media Works! (*http:www.inetworks.com*). The Web has already made money for her, both as an agent and as a Web site designer for clients like Pulte Corp. and Doyle Wilson Builders. She says:

> I personally sold a building site to a psychiatrist from Springfield, Illinois, who perused the Austin Real Estate Connection on the Web. On a whim during a holiday weekend he flew to Austin (without my company name or address or phone number) having only my last name and began to try to track me down. He found several Andersons who begged for his business, but he was adamant about working with the person who was smart enough to advertise on the Internet. I was out of town, but he simply enjoyed the visit to Austin and returned at a time more convenient for me and I sold him a lot within two days. Everything was closed by email except

CONTACT

T. J. Anderson
Internet Media Works
http://www.inetworks
tja@bga.com

for the final signature on documents. Today he is a valued friend and client with whom I exchange Internet marketing ideas.

The Web site I did for Doyle Wilson Homebuilder has generated approximately 7,000 hits per week. The site is very in-depth with a searchable floorplan database and walk-throughs on 21 models. During the IBM Boca Raton relocation to Austin, eight IBM employees in one day walked into Doyle Wilson subdivisions with downloaded floorplans in hand stating which house they wanted to buy. The response to the site has been overwhelming and feedback from customers is great. One guy wrote to a smaller builder site we created (because the builder just didn't believe the Net would work) and told the builder point-blank that while he appreciated his customer service efforts to advertise on the Net, his site was absolutely worthless to him and he should look at Doyle Wilson's site to see what a valuable builder's site should be. He said he could really shop for homes on that site and had all the information required to make his decision.

CCIM FORUMS

T. J. says the CCIM Commercial Real Estate Network (*http://www. ccim.com*) offers "the most interactive format of information sharing to date," with ten discussion forums for marketing commercial properties, discussion of commercial real estate industry news, and Web news and uses in commercial real estate. Also offered is information about financing, market trends and international networking, aimed at both real estate professionals and the general public. "Wonderful relationships have been forged in this interactive environment," T. J. says.

SETTING UP NETWORKS

If you take even a superficial look at commercial real estate on the Web, you run into the name Ted Kraus, manager of a commercial real estate home page, a commercial real estate fax-on-demand service, an online BBS network called RealtyNet, along with eight newsgroups and an online commercial real estate service called the DealMakers Online.

Ted runs five Internet mailing lists/forums on commercial real estate, appraisal, finance and investment real estate. The commercial list offers a place to network and post press releases as well as commercial listings for sale or lease. To join the commercial real estate forum, send an email message to *listserv@property.com*. In the body of the message, type: **subscribecommercial-realestate** *your Internet address.*

Ted calls this little empire his "hobby" and claims that the way he puts food on the table is by leasing, brokering, selling and managing shopping centers, and publishing his hard copy *DealMakers* newsletter.

"We're a small company (11 employees)," says Ted, "but we work in 36 states. So when we're busy, we're very busy, but when we're slow, the overhead doesn't kill us."

PERSONAL ACCOUNT

Ted Kraus
The DealMakers
http://www.property.com/

ted.kraus@property.com

Building a Custom Network

Ted recently posted an open invitation on the DealMakers to brokers interested in forming a small integrated commercial referral network (obviously aimed at those whose grasp of technology includes email):

We're offered opportunities that we don't have the skills to handle which requires a different expertise than handling the sale or leasing of property in a major market, etc.

Therefore, I am attempting to start a network of real estate professionals (more formal than this list provides) who will work together, promote one another, provide referrals and take on assignments.

I picture it being made up of brokers representing major markets (i.e., one broker for Chicago, another for southern Illinois) and brokers for the minor markets. In addition, we would have experts for regions (north, east, west, south) on subjects such as 1031s, bankruptcies, accounting, phase ones, etc., the idea being that united we can provide our clients with better service and hopefully make more money for ourselves. We would split commissions or pay a referral fee based on the situation.

There are two major obstacles I see with this. One, for this to work, we need the best in each market (who knows how we determine that). Two, how many will want to join who will not really contribute or share information? In order for this to work, we have to have exclusives in the market, be in constant contact by email and phone, and meet at least every 4–6 months. So how do we determine who's real from who's not?

To eliminate those who join because they have nothing to lose, there has to be an initiation fee of some sort (say between $1,000–5,000) that at first would be placed into escrow and later used to promote the group and exhibit at various trade shows.

T J. Anderson comments:

Ted has a good idea here. In those many situations where brokers don't have exclusive listings, that could be a problem, though. If he took it to the

Internet, as I am trying to do, it might work. I think in a public forum style with experts as moderators for a live posting session (I am trying to get interested parties on the CCIM site to do something similar), the network could more easily establish itself on an international basis. If he started live CU-SeeMe-type conferencing for this purpose, it could be unique enough to work. Certainly the bandwidth issues will be solved pretty rapidly.

T. J., obviously reflecting her own present area of interest, sees the applications of Ted's idea as meeting a greater need in the international arena:

> We are starting to do that on our international forum on CCIM. Particularly in light of the wide reach of the Net, this should be taken several steps further, one being that there is a need for foreign language brokers to facilitate international deals and act as translators both verbally and culturally—I see the Internet making that more viable especially in a conferencing setting. I have signed a contract with Beijing, China, to construct a real estate and business information site to provide for the interactive dissemination of real estate and investment information for foreign investors. This is part of the dream—bringing diverse cultures together in an interactive environment with immediate access to information.
>
> Ari Feldman, CCIM, CIPS, spends lots of time in Mexico City and South America, and he is helping put together our international forum to facilitate this type of interaction in foreign markets. I would think international deals rather than U.S. deals would benefit most from what Ted is suggesting.

Greg Laycock says that just as the MLSs are now putting all their listings on the Web, commercial brokers, led by Ted and others, are following suit in relinquishing proprietary control over inventory that once forced customers to their door. "It stands to reason that a lot of people are not going to be in business," says Greg. "I can download population figures, income stats, and listing opportunities, so what's a broker going to do for me?"

Greg says he is positioning himself as a "knowledge synthesizer, someone who can help buyers understand why they should do this deal, help them with nuances of a specific market, help them perform the gut check. I can run internal rate of return estimates in the conference room. You're going to see a lot more brokers working other markets, being investment advisors and strategists working different markets for the same clients."

REAL ESTATE
INVESTMENT TRUSTS

The pressures of commoditization that many agents fear will come with commerce on the Internet are already a fact of life for real estate investment trusts, many of which are publicly traded and used to having investors judge them solely on the basis of FFO, dividends and net yield. To put it mildly, successful REITs—whose appeal to investors is the opportunity to invest in real estate without taking on management headaches or placing their entire investment in a single property—do not run their businesses by accident. An apartment REIT must know how to keep vacancies low and get the best available prices in replacing worn-out carpets and appliances if it wants to compete with its peers.

Real estate companies intent on making full use of the business communications and marketing potential of the Internet will take a page from real estate investment trusts like Kranzco, one of the REIT pioneers in serious Net commerce.

A COMPANY INTRANET

Kranzco Realty Investment Trust, headquartered in Conshohocken, Pennsylvania, has already gotten used to two important Net synergies: "intranet" communications for its internal operations and free Net advertising for tenants in the shopping centers Kranzco owns and manages. One of the first REITs on the Internet, the company has had a Web page since 1995.

Kranzco gets around 2,000 hits per week on its site. "I get a fair amount of email from brokers bringing properties to our attention," says Michael Kranzdorf, director of information systems at Kranzco, who serves on the ICSC Research Task Force and is working with NAREIT to set up an information systems working group.

Michael's wife Susan, a programmer and Kranzco's Webmaster, explained the kind of visits the Web site draws: "As a public company, Kranzco has many parties interested in its corporate information. Analysts, stockholders, prospective stockholders, real estate brokers looking for space for tenants and sellers of other shopping centers are all looking for specific data."

Kranzco now offers a unique Internet advertising benefit for tenants in its 38 shopping centers. Tenants are being offered free space on the World Wide Web to publicize their business, and may also include logos and additional information for a small fee.

"All of our tenants are currently listed by shopping center location on our Internet Web site," says Michael. "Visitors to our home page will find a wealth of information, including plot plans, tenant lists and available space for all of our centers, press releases, 10K and 10Q SEC filings." He says a number of tenants' home offices have inquired about more comprehensive use of the Web site.

Susan says the information systems department at Kranzco Realty Trust has accessed the Internet for several years. "We rely on newsgroups as well as mailing lists such as Oracle-L, and Apple-Internet for technical information relating to our work. These resources, among others, established the Internet as an integral part of our work environment early on. Once the World Wide Web started to became popular, it was natural for us to think of creating a page of our own."

Users of the Kranzco Web page find an interactive map of the northeastern United States showing locations of Kranzco's properties. A click of the mouse reveals a plot plan and tenant list for a given center. For interested tenants and brokers, available retail sites are shown.

Real estate brokers and principals with properties for sale can view Kranzco's current acquisition criteria. Analysts and investors can find recent 10K and 10Q SEC filings and all press releases issued during the past three years. All users can send mail directly to KRT through the Web site with comments or questions about any aspect of the company's operations.

PERSONAL ACCOUNT

Susan Kranzdorf
Kranzco REIT
http://www.krt.com

webmaster@mis.kirt.com

Web Site Security

All information provided on the Internet is publicly available from other sources. To maintain security, the Web site is not hosted in, nor connected to, the company's offices. Susan recalls:

> We first proposed the idea of creating a Web site for Kranzco in the spring of 1995, just as the Web started to gain popularity in the business world. At that time our president and CEO, Norman Kranzdorf (*nmk@krt.com*), asked securities analysts if they would use such a tool to gather information. The response at that time was basically, "The World Wide What?"
>
> Within months, however, the Web's presence became seemingly ubiquitous, and by summer, analysts along with everyone else were clamoring for sites to visit. I began to work full time on the project in September aiming to finish by October, in time for an official unveiling at a National Association of Real Estate Investment Trusts (NAREIT) conference. We already had an Internet Service Provider and knew that using them to host the site would speed completion of the project considerably.

REITwatch

http://www.review.net

The best Web source about REITs is ReviewNet's REITwatch, which tracks REITs that operate in Florida. REITwatch offers contact information, book value per share of stock, and total market value of each company. Each company gets a short review.

As one of the company's database programmers, Susan was able to see that her work on the Web site put her in a position to develop the next generation of Kranzco intracompany communications:

> I have done some work on providing an "intranet" to the office, a server set up in the office to provide the same kinds of information formatted in HTML, internally to KRT workers. In addition, there are already many tools that help in the creation of HTML front ends to relational databases. We see this as an attractive future. Tying the site to data from our corporate relational database facilitates keeping the site up to date, minimizes the effort required to add new data and allows tremendous flexibility. We see the popularity and usefulness of the World Wide Web continuing to blossom as technology improves.

Kranzco owns and operates 38 shopping centers with 5.7 million square feet in Connecticut, Maryland, New Jersey, New York, Pennsylvania, Rhode Island and Virginia. The trust, formed in 1992, owns 5,700,000 square feet of retail space and has assets of over $440,000,000.

WISHES THEY WOULD CATCH UP

S. R. (Steve) Wicker is one who believes the real estate market will change drastically under the consumer-driven pressures of the Web. "I have a lot of experience in this area," he says. "I have always been told that I was five years ahead of my time. Like Willie Nelson, I wish they would catch up so we could all earn some money!"

TEN31 is linked to and affiliated with other sites we have visited: the DealMakers, the Home Port, Warfield's Florida Review (publisher of REITwatch), in addition to sites like Investors Network Publishing, Nationwide 1031 Exchange Services, Property Information Exchange, and Real Estate Investments Online. TEN31's members include investors as well as agents.

Wicker's former company, Realty Mart, REALTORS, began a guaranteed sales program in 1966 and went on to do more than 3,000 such sales while most real estate salespeople never understood, let alone participated in, such transactions. He is used to being part of a minority of real estate agents using technology. A former president of the Louisiana Realtors Association, he fought the good fight to bring technology to real estate practice:

CONTACT

Seaborn Wicker
TEN31 Marketplace

http://www.ten31.com/

seaborn@ten31.com

> The electronic calculator was perhaps the most difficult thing to get a salesperson to use, especially to learn the key strokes necessary to compute loan payments. When creative financing came into being in the late 1970s

and early 1980s, teaching them to compute yields and structure wrap-around mortgages was almost impossible. In 1974 we introduced a computer to our more than 100 associates. We used the "Silent 700" Texas Instruments portable terminals. We would take it to a client's house, hook it to the telephone and call the computer. We could prepare a competitive market analysis, place listings on the market, qualify buyers, search for property, search for qualified buyers, financing, etc. Many of these tasks are still not being performed with today's sophisticated computers.

NET LENDERS

As real estate agents take to the Web, mortgage lenders find it more and more important to be there as well. Data security remains a concern for lenders and competitive conditions are not yet ripe for widespread acceptance. But some lenders, large and small, have already set up shop on the Web and begun to make themselves at home.

IS IT SECURE?

Though the notion of cybercash and Visa purchases at World Wide Web malls seems less exotic every day, this is not yet an everyday fact of life to most of us. Worries about Web security have received a great deal of media attention, despite the fact that, as attendees at a Glasser Legal-Works seminars on cyberbanking are reminded, the Web security system is essentially the same one that sheltered plans for the B-1 bomber.

FIGURE 11-1
ComSpace Internet Services was started to fill an underserved niche, small commercial spaces for lease. Though their pages for some cities are still sparse, they are growing. (http://www. comspace.com)

Firewall

An electronic security barrier that blocks unauthorized access to an online database.

Ina Bechhoefer says she is asked about Web security all the time. "I do see a hesitation on the part of consumers. People are skeptical," she says. Ina herself would be satisfied within six months to a year "if the firewalls are still working."

Ina suggests that if widespread doubts persist, third parties could guarantee the security of Web transactions or indemnify consumers in case of losses. She says concerns over the security of financial transactions on the Web are due in part to unfamiliarity.

Lingering Concerns

Lingering security concerns, valid or not, have made lenders (and title companies) think twice about using the Internet to take applications and transmit documents. One major exception to that general reluctance is Bank of America.

If, as Contour Software president Scott Cooley says, the Internet is forcing lenders to rethink marketing strategies, one of the reasons is that other lenders can't help noticing what Bank of America has done.

B of A, which established a major presence on the World Wide Web way back in mid-1994, was receiving about 600,000 hits per week by early 1996 on its various pages. B of A has established Web links to real estate agents in all 50 states. No other lender has yet achieved B of A's massive Web presence.

A number of lenders (many, like Norwest, PHH U.S. Mortgage, GE Capital, and North American Mortgage, with hot links to Homebuyer's Fair) are now on the Net. Contour's survey of 10 lenders shows that a Web page generates new mortgage customer leads as soon as it is launched. Dick Lepre at Homeowners Finance in California reports hundreds of inquiries a month. After two weeks on the Net, David Lusk of Ryland Mortgage in Georgia reported $1.8 million in mortgage leads and one application.

The Contour survey shows why the stampede of commerce to the Net will continue unabated: "The survey revealed that the Internet is about as good as print in generating mortgage leads, However, advertising on the Internet is considerably cheaper than print." And all accounts seem to agree that the Internet beats all other media in generating mortgage originations for relocation buyers.

People don't have to surf around looking for Bank of America—or even intend to reach its home page before they get there—because so many sites have swapped hyperlinks with B of A. Bank of America's "Online Listings " pages for individual states across the nation are linked (for free) to real estate marketing services and local brokerages, which in turn are linked back to B of A's site for home financing

CONTACT

Karen Shapiro
Bank of America
http://www.bankamerica. com

webmaster@bankamerica. com

Alltel and Five Paces

http://www.fivepaces.com

Alltel Information Services and Five Paces, Inc., have joined to allow for companies around the world to offer their customers secure financial services on the Internet, utilizing the Secure Web Platform software. SecureWare is the developer of the trusted operating system technology used by the U.S. Department of Defense.

information. To find out how to link up with Bank of America, email the B of A Webmaster. Only offices and listing services with a significant number of listings will be accepted, says B of A.

B of A's enhanced "At Home" page is accessed from "Personal Finance." The latest edition of the Netscape browser now permits a home buyer to fill out a loan application, allows prospective borrowers to determine what home prices they can afford, compute monthly payments, and run "what if" scenarios on fixed vs. variable rate loans.

A list of criteria lenders use in evaluating a loan, a glossary of home terms, information on closing costs, tips on evaluating the condition of a home—all help prospective borrowers become more informed about the process.

Bank of America vice president Karen Shapiro, product manager for the company's interactive marketing unit, says that 75–80 percent of the design and content for the B of A Web pages was done in-house, with outside vendors providing page layout and HTML.

She is particularly proud of the "What price home can I afford?" feature of the "At Home" page, which allows visitors to qualify themselves using actual B of A criteria. "A lot of people have something like that on their sites," says Karen, "but on ours if you give us the right information we'll give you the real answer."

Karen designed the home page itself and tested it to make sure it downloaded in under a minute for a computer selecting the page for the first time with a 14,400-baud modem. She even "torture tested" it with an old 2400-baud modem, bringing up the page in 3-1/2 minutes the first time and 15 seconds thereafter.

"We really designed the site to repeat the banner graphics to conserve bandwidth," she says, emphasizing that making sure visitors move quickly and smoothly from one feature of the site to the next is a B of A obsession. Like other lenders, she noted that a significant number of the serious mortgage enquiries B of A receives come from people relocating to another state.

Not all visitors to the B of A Web site come to shop; two thirds of the visits are accessed from commercial servers, while one third come from educational servers.

What comes next for Bank of America on the Net is to consolidate, harvest what the company has already sown, and concentrate on electronic banking. "1995 was difficult because nobody had done it before. By 1996, everybody knew a little and everyone wanted to get on," Karen says.

GIVING BORROWERS A BREAK

Dick Lepre of HomeOwners Finance Center, a California mortgage broker, has a network of 27 agents across the country linked together to accept online mortgage loan applications.

Thanks to his affiliation with HomeOwners Finance, Christopher Munzo—a licensed mortgage broker with P. A. Mortgage Services Inc. in Florida—competes head to head with Bank of America on the World Wide Web. Both B of A and Chris have 1,003 residential mortgage applications on their Web sites; both B of A and Chris must be very sure those applications are secure.

But B of A requires that the customary fee be filed with the application. Not only don't the HomeOwners affiliated brokers charge a fee, they offer a $250 discount to borrowers making their applications over the Internet.

Because P. A. Mortgage in Florida is not (yet) computerized, applications emailed to Chris Munzo actually go to HomeOwners and are then faxed from California back to Florida, creating a quaint bump in HomeOwners' otherwise highly sophisticated operations.

Chris (unlike B of A) spent only $300 on his Web site, which nevertheless offers full convenience to the visitor. He says, "People can enter my Web page and prequalify themselves for a loan by answering a few simple questions. I then communicate via email or by phone and follow up on the details. From the standpoint of competition, I really don't feel threatened by anyone else on the Net. On the Net, I appear to be as important as Citicorp or Norwest."

P. A. Mortgage is a small office that bills itself as "Florida's Premier Lender." Chris Munzo has been with them for the past two years, having worked before that for Core States Financial in Philadelphia as a financial institutions representative.

FIGURE 11-2

HomeOwners Finance Center (http://www.homeowners.com)

In one typical week at P. A. Mortgage, Chris says, he received "three loan application packages from around the state of Florida that come to me strictly because of the World Wide Web. Better yet, they all included the check for the appraisal and credit report. Two refinances and a purchase on the East Coast (I'm in Tampa) and I've only spoken to one of the three applicants; the other two have been email correspondence only." He says the non-believers in his office have begun to ask questions about the Internet.

Chris was the only loan officer at P. A. Mortgage really comfortable with computers. He himself does not own a laptop and only works at home in the mornings to avoid rush hour traffic and answer his email. Though he has a desktop computer at work, his online operations are left behind once he leaves home.

If visitors to his Web page are worried about the security of the application, they don't express those concerns to him. "I have yet to have anyone say they saw the application, but didn't feel comfortable about filling it out. There are people who send me the application all filled out before they even email or phone me, though."

When Chris explains loan products, his experience and expertise show through. In his message to Web visitors he steps right up and offers clear informed counsel:

> P. A. Mortgage Service has over twenty-five wholesale investors that offer loan programs through us. Part of my job is to study those programs and find the best one for you. Most of our loans are offered with zero points [a point is 1% of your loan amount], although you can improve your rate if you are willing to pay one or more points.
>
> A word of caution about 15-year fixed rates: I do not like them!!! Why would you contractually obligate yourself to a higher payment? You are sacrificing your liquidity and putting a needless strain on your cash flow. Your money works harder for you in the bank or in a mutual fund than it does in your house. If you really want to pay off that house early, get a 30-year loan and pay extra each month—you'll accomplish the same thing!!!

Though Chris has no formal alliances with real estate agents, he works with Mark Pope of Prudential Florida Realty. One transaction they did together was the sale and purchase loan for a civilian military employee living in Germany who found both his real estate agent and loan agent by surfing the Internet.

Mark's Web page looks a lot like Chris's because, says Chris, Mark "stole my background." If you have not yet seen an online CMA, by the way, check out Mark's site (*http://www.fl realestate.com*).

Dick Lepre in San Francisco says HomeOwners Finance Center would have at least one agent in every state "within two weeks" if he could take time away from his own mortgage business to work the phones and canvas Internet newsgroups.

Chris says one reason HomeOwners has not yet signed up loan brokers in all fifty states is that Dick Lepre charges a modest $150 a month to help support his costs to advertise with the Yahoo and Lycos search engines many people use to shop for real estate on the Web. "It's worth it to me," says Chris, "Dick has already sent me three deals that closed."

While acknowledging that B of A offers customers a lot of convenient services, Dick says HomeOwners Financial "does the exact opposite: we say to the borrower, 'You do all the work and get a price break in return.'"

The increased automation brought to the mortgage process by Fannie Mae and Freddie Mac is "setting up systems that eliminate the vast majority of the tasks that we do," says Dick. "The lending business is going to become so automated and streamlined that there is going to be a lot more price competition. If these things can be done for almost nothing, borrowers are going to benefit enormously."

Dick enjoys playing David vs. Goliath by undercutting mortgage fees charged by his larger competitors. A computer consultant since the Sixties (who calls himself "a humble loan officer"), Dick got into the mortgage business by way of his consulting work for Continental Savings & Loan.

He says the Web "has enabled me to do loans over a greater geographical area. Now I can much more readily do loans all over the state. When the borrower is somebody in San Francisco and I go to get their loan application at their house, that's one thing. But if I am doing business with people I don't actually meet face to face, it really doesn't matter where they are in the state. I order an appraisal and so on, and deal with them the same way no matter how many miles away they are."

Dick proclaims flatly, "We have the best financial site of all." Recent additions to the HomeOwners prize-winning site are a "Refi TestDrive, where you can instantly compare your current loan to ours" and an "Economic Calendar" highlighting important economic events.

Dick actually fathered the strategy of online applications and of offering real estate loan shoppers a $250 rebate. He says that amount may need adjustment to make economic sense in states where loan amounts tend to be much smaller than in California.

BAY BANK SOLUTIONS

We've talked about interactivity and how important it is to a Web page. Bay Bank Solutions (*http://BayBank.com*) offers customized answers to questions about loans that incorporate enquirers' responses to a set of questions and translate them into customized answers to loan needs.

Visitors to the site can fill out a questionnaire describing their real estate and mortgage needs. Bay Bank then uses composite sketches of actual borrowers to illustrate real-life options. The effect is to allow prospective borrowers an ingenious way to "discuss" their mortgage needs with the Web page. Using a variety of calculators provided, including a Closing Cost Calculator, customers can go on to explore the financial implications of a home purchase and then either ask for a mail-in loan worksheet or email back the less extensive online version.

Whichever way prospects choose to respond, Bay Bank rewards them with a coupon for $100 off closing costs. Giving money back is always a welcome way to encouage interactivity.

Chapter *12* A Look at the Future

Mr. Broker pushes the buttons on his video phone. This links him directly to the central computer, which takes five seconds to scan all the properties in the location desired. A printed sheet then comes out of the side of the phone with the names of four properties that fit his needs. Each of these properties is analyzed as to how it will affect Mr. Investor's tax and growth pictures.

By pushing a separate button on the phone, Mr. Broker then activates a videotape which projects over a small screen next to the phone. The investor is able to sit in the comfort of the agent's office and view the exterior, lobby, sample rental units, boiler room and neighborhood of the four properties already selected and analyzed. If he wants to fly out and see the property in person, the instrument on Mr. Broker's desk can even make his reservations and print the airline ticket on the spot!

▶ The Vision

▶ Electronic Signatures and Paperless Transactions

▶ Commoditization of the Web

▶ Revolutionary Changes

THE VISION

Commercial investment technology guru Jack Peckham wrote those words on the prior page (quoted most recently in the *Commercial Investment Real Estate Journal*) back in 1968. They still stand as a benchmark for the use of technology in the marketplace. Just as printer drivers in a Windows environment do their work in the background while the computer user is free to go ahead and work on other tasks instead of waiting for a document to print out, ease of access and use are the aim of every developer of Web-related technology. Customers can point a mouse here, push a button there, and get whatever they came looking for.

Jack says that, early on, commercial brokers used technology for analysis rather than marketing, but that many are now starting to embrace all forms of technology in their business. T. J. Anderson predicts that commercial practitioners will begin to keep pace with their residential colleagues:

CONTACT

John M. "Jack" Peckham III, CCIM
The Peckham Boston Advisory Company
http://www.inetworks. com/revest

75162.360@ compuserve.com

You will see many changes in the use of the Web in the next 12–24 months, particularly in the areas of peer-to-peer networking using Windows 95 via the Internet, Java, VRML, plug-ins, and browser capability. Offices, brokers, and clients can share files directly from their own computers as though they were in the same office as long as they have taken the minimal time to configure Windows 95 to use the Internet Gateway interface that allows recognition of another computer. This is a relatively simple thing to do and basically provides the largest wide area network (WAN) in the world. For example, say you, another broker in Mexico City, and one in Japan are working on a project — putting marketing information together, gathering stats, etc. Of course, you could email the information back and forth until you get it just right, but using the Internet as a WAN, you can access Word documents, graphics and spreadsheets on each other's computers instantly—using the Internet through your own local access provider to funnel the information at no cost. Documents on all computers are accurately updated at all times. This is a particularly important use of the Net for individual or small office brokers as well as large corporations.

Karen Shapiro, Bank of America's Webmaster, expects to offer B of A video-conferencing directly from the Internet. That adventure awaits a technological great leap forward, but she says B of A will be an early leaper when the opportunity comes.

The visions people still look forward to achieving for the sale of real estate on the Net differ only in a few details from the picture Jack Peckham painted in 1968. Here is a composite of several such visions:

FIGURE 12-1
*"Real Estate
Investments On Line"
(http://www.
inetworks.com/revest)*

CONTACT

Karen Shapiro
Bank of America
*http://www.bankamerica.
com*

*webmaster@bankamerica.
com*

Our prospective buyers—having come to realize that unmonitored free virtual tours of homes for sale always begin through a doorway marked "Caveat Emptor"—pay a small fee to take a more professional and reliable virtual tour. The three online listings they will tour are selected according to criteria that buyer, agent and tour vendor agree closely match the buyers' prestated criteria and financial qualifications.

As the prospective buyers approach the house, their virtual guide's voice welcomes them and alerts them that waiting inside the house are a pest inspector, a contractor, an interior decorator, a financial services provider, an attorney and Larry, their Smart Guide driver in case they want to tour the local area after they've seen the house. Like genies, all these advisors stay out of sight and (until asked to comment) charge our homeseekers nothing.

After taking a first virtual walk through the house, the buyers decide they want to have the contractor give them an estimate on converting the attic to an additional bedroom. The contractor starts the meter running for the consultation (first giving notice of per-minute rate) and a Contractor's Report window pops up in the lower right corner of the monitor screen. Already highlighted are flashing hypertext warnings to check local building codes governing remodeling and to consult with a pest inspector. The buyers continue walking upstairs to the attic, and the contractor answers their questions about building a dormer window and adding skylights.

Before making a hyperlink invitation to have the interior decorator give them a short consultation, they press the Local Codes button on the contractor's report and take a quick look at the restrictions, zoning limitations and fees they would face if they went forward with their remodeling idea. They press the Pest Inspection button on the Contractor's Report and a Red Flag notice comes up informing them that the house has been treated with methyl bromide for an infestation of wood-boring beetles. They also receive a list of termite repairs made (including some new joists in the attic) and a price for a reinspection.

Having satisfied themselves that the house still meets their criteria for a "nicer little fixer-upper with room for expansion and plenty of charm and potential," our buyers give the hyperlink command for the decorator to come up to the attic and toss in some quick money-making ideas.

Is this how value-added relationships will work for real estate sales on the World Wide Web of the future? How likely is it that such a scenario could be achieved any time soon? What are the barriers? What other Web wonders await the real estate community?

Though people are not going to buy homes they don't visit in person, Scott Cooley predicts that some aspects of the above scenario will take place fairly soon: "Video clips and photos of the house will soon become standard on the Net. Years from now, we may be able to view the neighborhood. However, photos and even video will never replace actually being there." Scott questions some points in detail:

The idea of contractors and decorators working in a virtual world is questionable. For example, where would all of the exact dimensions come from? We might be able to show rooms in different paint and carpet and may get to the point where furniture can be moved around and decorations placed in a virtual home.

However, this would be using standard types of furniture and certainly couldn't be items the buyer already owns (unless the buyer had a digital camera). Information already gathered, including images of documents, can certainly be accessible (i.e., termite report).

A big limiting factor is that building plans on homes are not accessible electronically, with no way in the near future to have them done. This prevents things like a deck or a room addition from being reality because no dimensions are known.

I also doubt that buyers would ever pay for these services until after deciding to purchase the house. Initial house hunting will always be considered free and the agents wishing to sell houses will be offering Web house-hunting services just like they do now.

Scott also offers a reminder that some information not mentioned in the scenario is either available on the Internet right now or will be soon, such as economic information about towns, states, and countries, computerized statistical appraisals, data about environmental hazards, and financing options.

Arnold Kling of Homebuyer's Fair is skeptical about the Web as a place to shop for homes:

I think that the Web is primarily a research and communications tool, but as a presentation medium it falls well short of magazines and TV, and even farther short of reality. I think that the message I would convey to agents is that the Web is going to replace the Yellow Pages and newspaper classified ads. People are going to use the Web to replace these tools because of its richer search capabilities, greater depth of information, and easier ways to obtain information about another city. It's going to be necessary for an agent to have a Web listing, just as today it is necessary to be listed in the phone book and to have ads in print publications. I expect that real estate agents will re-allocate their advertising budgets away from print and toward the Web.

Mary Kay Aufrance says she and her husband Tom love to regale students in their seminars with stories of virtual tours and marketing wonders the Web will provide for real estate sales. However, they say, the Internet itself is not cutting-edge technology. Economic as well as technical constraints on bandwidth, for one, put the brakes on what the Web now can offer:

The coolest thing will be using your Web browser on your color laptop while on tour with a buyer—to find homes in the buyer's interest area and narrowing down before driving all over town—then to get info on homes as you drive by. Plus, wait till Internet phone allows you to call, see and talk to the listing agent as you sit outside the home wanting more information!

When I paint this kind of picture during presentations, people really like it. However, although the Internet is considered high-tech and cutting-edge technology, as software developers, Tom and I see it as a refreshingly simple de-evolution in the world of development tools. The whole medium is built on sending simple ASCII text characters and a few graphics and audio file formats around on phone lines.

The simplicity of this medium has obviously stumped some developers, Microsoft included, who are having a hard time presenting interesting and useful applications within the confines imposed by the simple set of tools available for development. This is why we aren't seeing the entire JC Penney catalog online and aren't able to cyber-walk around in mansions for sale on the Mendocino coast. In fact, the Internet may never be the best medium for either of these activities.

(The simplicity of the Internet as a software development platform is also why Microsoft is at work to "complexify" things as fast as it can—why would we need to buy any more software if we didn't have to use their really spiffy but too-GUI "productivity" tools?)

GUI (graphical user interface)

A pictoral point and click screen environment. for example, Windows is a GUI.

I think the Internet will continue to be a tool that challenges the extravagant and satisfies those creative enough to develop interesting presentations and applications with minimal technology!

ELECTRONIC SIGNATURES AND PAPERLESS TRANSACTIONS

TitleLink president Jody Lane says he has no trouble believing that electronic home tours will be possible, with or without various vendors "standing by" to offer advice on demand the way lenders have loan officers standing by at loan centers right now to take applications via teleconferencing. His reservations about the composite scenario offered above is that it doesn't address the most crucial impacts of technology. Jody says:

I have no problem imagining video shopping, because I just looked at a Corvette on the Internet myself. Somebody might offer home shoppers online consulting, though I don't see some of the services mentioned as being very practical. But let's face it, there is a coolness in some technology that makes you throw it in and play with it because it is fun. My problem with the virtual home tour scenario is twofold. First of all, if the implication is supposed to be that people are going to buy homes sight unseen over the Internet, I don't believe that for a second. People will shop on the Web but they won't buy homes that way. They will continue to purchase their homes the same way they do right now, by using the services of a real estate agent they trust and spending a lot of time looking at real houses before they make an offer on one.

We are already witnessing the "power agents"—those real estate agents who are closing more volume and making more money than ever before. They are using all current technology available to them to handle this increased volume, and the reason they have the increased volume is because this technology makes them look smarter and more professional. The future looks bright indeed for them.

The second objection I have is that the scenario doesn't address the transaction logjams that technology and the Internet can be used to solve in the future. Those occur after the offer is made and accepted, not before. The slowdown in a real estate transaction is that Freddie Mac can get an answer back on a loan in minutes with Loan Prospector, but we still take six weeks to close an escrow. Why? Why can't I have an appraisal on your home in fifteen minutes? Why can't I get title insurance the same day I order it? These are the developments technology has in store for us.

The acceptance of electronic signatures and the coming of the paperless transaction are miracles awaiting us, and by the year 2005 you'll absolutely have those things. Those represent enormously powerful changes in the way we focus the power of technology to make the world work better.

PERSONAL ACCOUNT

**Jeremy McCarty
SRA Appraisals**

Stored Appraisals

Appraiser Jeremy McCarty of SRA says the appraisal process will indeed speed up:

There are two major forces that will dramatically change the appraisal industry in the near future, and both are a result of recent technological and communication advances. The first force is the reduction in the need for appraisals on certain property and loan types. With the advent of sophisticated loan underwriting and risk analysis systems, lenders can complete a loan transaction without an appraisal. Fannie Mae and Freddie Mac have designed systems to allow for this, and in the future this type of transaction should comprise a certain percentage of all loans funded. Artificial intelligence and regression analysis programs will also be viable means for determining a value or level of risk that, if coupled with a quick property inspection, will replace the need for a full appraisal.

The second force is the result of advances in electronic communication and transfer of information. The electronic standard format for an appraisal has recently been developed which will eventually allow any appraiser to electronically deliver an appraisal to any client. We believe this will enable appraisers to service nationwide clients rather than primarily being restricted to a local clientele as has been typical to date. Although the need for some of the services appraisers have traditionally provided will diminish, other services are likely to become required as certain technologies become available and affordable. These services might include a variety of consulting services made available on the Internet or other platforms to the public, real estate agents, attorneys, lenders, etc.; inspection services which may involve video imaging and real-time conferencing and information transfer; and electronic marketing and service alliances with other real estate industry service providers such as title companies, home inspectors, real estate agents, etc.

It is very likely that access to these technologies will be in one form or another via secure Internet channels and much of the advertising, communication and delivery of appraisal services will also occur on the Internet of the not so distant future.

COMMODITIZATION OF WEB SERVICES

Commoditization pressures on Web-related real estate services will continue, says Tom Aufrance:

CONTACT

Tom Aufrance
Aufrance Associates
http://www.highsierra.com
tmaufr@highsierra.com

> A couple of our agents have already tried the "specials" angle: $250 off of escrow fees, for example. This is probably not a big enough inducement to produce much buyer excitement.
>
> A price sheet for sellers makes the most sense. They're already paying the bill anyway and you could probably break down selling costs into sensible categories: $X/month to advertise your home in print media, $Y/month for Internet marketing services, $Z for "ad" campaign design and management, $A for escrow supervision, $B for negotiation/arbitration services, $C for marketing analysis, and so on.
>
> Buyer's agents would probably charge hourly for chauffeur services with flat rate charges for negotiation and escrow services as well. As soon as a generally understood menu of services is established, then price wars would inevitably follow. Consumers would be more satisfied as they better understand the services they're paying for ("Just what is my agent doing to sell my house?")
>
> How could this happen in the face of entrenched resistance? It would probably require a national franchise organization to take the lead, like Charles Schwab did with the discount stockbroker idea. Sellers would be induced to sign up if their costs were reduced because they're not financing buyer's agents. Buyers would balk because they have to pay for what is a freebie in the MLS system. Seems like a tough nut to crack…today, anyway!

REVOLUTIONARY CHANGES

California real estate consultant Ted Tagami recalls that the Net's capability to offer information on demand and create mini-intranets is meant to serve ever cheaper and more powerful personal computers. Ted says:

CONTACT

Ted Tagami
Real Estate
Communications
ted@re.com

> I liken the revolutionary changes happening in business today as suddenly having the equivalent of a steering wheel and pedals for every computer terminal. What does this mean? It means we have the potential to easily reach out to our prospective homebuyers and sellers 24 hours a day, 7 days a week. They've got the steering wheel now. It means they can identify properties that interest them without the need of our assistance. It

means they can shop for a loan without first speaking with a bank, savings and loan, or mortgage broker.

It also means we can process efficiently. Title company couriers may all but disappear. Pest reports won't be tying up your fax line. Market analysis can be performed faster and with greater detail. It is only limited by our willingness to be creative and ask: how can I be more effective?

There are many components to this revolution. In the broadest sense, they are computing power, software development, bandwidth and deregulation.

In 1965, Gordon Moore, a cofounder of Intel, predicted that the transistor density of semiconductor chips would double every 18 months. This is known as Moore's Law and has held true to this day. This means that the machine that would fill a building in 1965 sits on your desktop today. In other words, what we use today is more than 2 million times more powerful as in 1965.

New software is being developed literally daily for this new networked world. With Netscape plug-ins and alliances with companies like Sun with their Java programming, the Microsoft paradigm is up for grabs. Software doesn't even need to exist on your machine anymore. That's what Larry Ellison at Oracle has in mind when he talks about his network computer.

At this feverish pace, text has begun to disappear and is being replaced with graphics, animation, executable programs, sound and video. What does this mean to us? Supply and demand. Every company that offers connectivity (telco, cable, etc.) is rushing to provide greater capacity to handle the increased demand in bandwidth. Enter: the telecommunications reform bill, to set the stage for the Infobahn everyone keeps telling you is here.

In a nutshell, where does all this leave agents? Well, for the cost of an average commission, one can invest in more computing power than it took to send Neil Armstrong to the moon.

User interfaces are getting easier. I've just recently been enjoying the beta of a screen saver product called Pointcast (*www.pointcast.com*). Forget the flying toasters and fish tanks. This is a screen saver that receives updated news and weather feeds as well as stock updates via the Internet. Just point and click to retrieve the latest information. Look for a real estate application like this in the near term.

Where will the real estate industry be in five years? I don't know if I could tell you where it will be *next* year!

Internet trainer Michael Russer says:

The future promise and possibilities of the Internet hinge a great deal on the capabilities of the infrastructure that carries the data between computers. Today's highest modem speed of 33,600 bps is still far too slow for some of the more anticipated Net applications, such as full-motion color video. However, in the very near future (two to three years), cable modems with speeds 1,000 or more times faster than today's fastest analog modems will become widely available and allow us to be connected 24 hours a day. At this speed, the telephone and much of TV and radio will become nearly obsolete. It is hard to imagine just how our personal and business lives will change with that level of connectivity.

Will the World Wide Web fulfill T. J. Anderson's dreams for it? She says so:

> I can say that my dreams for dissemination of information within the real estate community and the public both locally and internationally are already being met. For the first time in history there is a unique relationship forming between all entities involved in a real estate transaction, and I see the possibility of totally facilitating a real estate deal via the Internet. In fact, this is already happening for some of us in the commercial real estate industry.
>
> The future is what we make it, and the Internet education process we are all currently involved in will help facilitate that dream. Actually, not knowing exactly how the dream will play out is the challenge. New technology is appearing hourly, and the public knowledge is growing at such a rate that anything is possible. Practice may be a different thing! There is no doubt in my mind that the way real estate is practiced in 1996 is not real estate practice as we will know it at the end of this century.

Though I can't predict how the Internet will shape your business, I can predict that real estate agents like T. J. Anderson who have embraced the Net are creating the model of success for those real estate agents who follow. As is always the case with emerging technologies, those who embrace them early on will also be the first to benefit from them. Those who embrace them afterwards will benefit from their experience. And those who never embrace them will wither in the heat of competition.

I hope reading this book means you'll be among the former, rather than the latter.

Net Tips: A Dip Into the Rushing Web Stream

You need to get as comfortable as possibly, as quickly as possible, about turning to the Internet as your first source of information— because the chances are very good that whatever you're looking for is out there in some form. The following list of Web sites doesn't attempt to be a complete guide, but it hits crucial bases for your journey into the amazing real estate resources offered by the World Wide Web. WARNING: The author of this list makes no promises or warranties that any of these sites will still be in existence or located at these addresses when you go take a look. It's a fast-changing world out there.

MAKING YOUR OWN WEB PAGES

Sausage Software Co.

http://www.sausage.com

Hot Dog from Sausage Software in Australia; piggybacks on top of your already-installed Web browser by creating an icon to click when you want to see how your page looks when it's loaded.

Wilson Internet Services

http://www.garlic.com/rfwilson/webmarket/

Wilson Internet Services, a rich source of information and ideas on Internet marketing.

Online Marketing Discussion Group

http://www.popco.com/hyper/internet-marketing/

Archives and resources for Internet marketing discussion lists.

Help from CompuServe

http://www.ourworld.com

CompuServe's Web site for Personal Home Pages gives similar help.

Prodigy Personal Home Page

http://pages.prodigy.com/

Prodigy, through their Personal Web Pages, allows subscribers to set up home pages on the Net.

Domain Name Services

http://www.netbistro.com/synaptic/domain.html

Register your domain name. Lets you check which Internet domain names are still available.

Link Up to Other Sites

http://www.mgroup.com/freelinks/

Helps you publicize your own site.

An On-line Tool Box

http://www.iTools.com/

Itools is a nice interface to all kinds of search engines plus useful tools writers in the "Research-It" section (dictionaries, thesauri, translators, and lots more).

Get Your Site Listed

http://www.submit-it.com

Submit It! is a free service designed to make the process of submitting your URLs to a variety of Web catalogs faster and easier. Register with more than 15 different catalogs by filling out just one form.

MORE SEARCH TOOLS

All-in-one Search Engine

http://www.stpt.com/

Starting Point. Just what it says. Gets you to all the search engines.

Another Central Search Site

http://www.search.com/

C/net's Search.Com similarly lets you search well-known sites such as Yahoo, Excite, InfoSeek, Alta Vista, and other specialized sites from one easy-to-use search location.

A Topics List

http://www.w3.org/pub/WWW/

World Wide Web Consortium topic list.

LISTING SERVICES

Internet MLS

http://www.trinet.com.homeconn.Information.html

Home Connections, lists homes for sale.

On-line Real Estate Auctions

http://www.valleynet.com/~webcity/

The Real Estate Junction, real estate listings by category.

On-line East Coast

http://www.infi.net/REWeb

Real Estate Web, East Coast listings.

Electronic Realty Services

http://www.tyrell.net/~ers

Electronic Realty Services. Listings of apartments, houses, agents, commercial properties across the country. Offers both free and paid listings.

RE/Max Realty

http://www.remaxhq.com/atlanta

RE/Max North Atlanta's online service. Includes local listings and consumer information on buying and selling property in Georgia. Provides direct email to agents, mortgage lenders, home warranty providers, insurance agents, home inspectors, and attorneys.

FractalNet

http://www.fractals.com/realestate.html

FractalNet Real Estate Server, "the most complete ordered listing of residential real estate on the Internet." Fractal gives up-to-date information, online real estate listings, etc. Submit listing link request via email.

Buyer's Agent Network

http://www. bestagents.com.

Agents for Buyers Network provides information for buyers seeking agents to represent them exclusively.

Relocation Services

http://www.sover.net/~relo/

American Relocation Center, offers an array of tools.

National Listings

http://www.us-digital.com/homeweb

Includes nationwide listings, profiles of real estate companies and agents, financing and mortgage information, and consumer tips. Operated by U.S. Digital Corp., a publisher for the relocation and real estate industries.

For Sale by Owner

http://www.human.com/mkt/fsbo/

For Sale by Owner magazine. A place where owners can post their own ads, buyers can view listings, and agents can work the FSBO market.

Worldwide Listings

htp://www.wren.com

WRENet, World Real Estate Network, interactive and searchable real estate database, all kinds of property.

NEWS AND INFORMATION

According to Moninger

http://www.islandtime.com/index.html

Dave Moninger's Island Time, a real estate Web site packed with information, including a Web primer for real estate agents which offers important basics.

Appraisal Services

http://www.hway.net/rossman/alink.htm

Rossman & Mohring Appraisal Service. Contains valuable hints on submitting Web page URLs to get free links.

Nerd World

http://www.nerdworld.com/users/dstein/nw147.html

Nerd World Real Estate. Access to a plethora of real estate resources and sites.

Real Estate Software

http://mmink.com/re/contmanag.html

The Complete Real Estate Software Catalog, "the largest selection of real estate software and related products available anywhere."

Real Estate Law

http://lycos-tmp2.psc.edu/gifs/reviews/8_23_004.htm

Realty Law Network. Geared toward the professional. The list of hotlinks to real estate shopping sites is remarkable.

Appraisal Institute

http://www.realworks.com/ai

The Appraisal Institute's home page. Consumers can find local members of the institute and scroll through a real estate library.

Mortgage Rates

http://www.hsh.com

Information on mortgage rates from HSH Associates, which does extensive surveying nationwide. Includes well-informed commentary on matters affecting interest rates.

Fannie Mae

http://www.fanniemae.com

Federal National Mortgage Association site. Provides information on mortgages and related subjects.

On-line Forms

http://www.unitedsystems.com.

United Systems offers an array of computer-generated business forms, including forms for Realtors, appraisers, etc.

REITWATCH On-line

http://www.review.net/RealEstate/REIT/nflist.html

ReviewNet's REITWATCH, information compiled on 89 real estate investment trusts that own property in Florida. Many of them are major players in other states as well.

Cohousing On-line

http://seclab.cs.ucdavis.edu/~stanifor/cohousing.html

Cohousing information source. A type of collaborative housing that attempts to overcome the alienation of modern subdivisions. Popular in some designs for senior communities.

Easy Reading

http://c/net.com

Internet magazine with a wealth of tips and information. Go here to quickly get comfortable with the broader world of the Net.

Easy Surfing

http://gnn.com/wr/

Web Review, an online magazine that scans Net subjects with an informing and critical eye.

Facts on File

http://www.lexis-nexis.com

LEXIS-NEXIS Communications Center.

LENDERS AND REAL ESTATE SERVICES

Private Notes

http://www.charisworks.com/

Buys private notes; useful in carry-back situations.

Mortgage Information

http://www.interest.com/mortgagemkt.html

Mortgage Market Information Services. A wonderful resource for info on mortgage loans.

GE Capital On-line

http://www/ge.com/gec/index/htel

GE Capital, provides financial services, including loans.

Loan Calculators On-line

http:/www.homeowners.com/homeowners/index.html

Home mortgage loans, calculator, Refi Testdrive.

Car Loans, and More

http://www.financenter.com/index.html

Financenter, an awarding-winning easy-to-use site for home loans, car loans, credit cards, etc. If you're shopping, this is a good spot to check out.

Lenders Meet Borrowers

http://www.loanlist.com

American mortgage listings, brings lenders and borrowers together.

WINDOW-SHOP THE WEB WITH YOUR CUSTOMERS

By now I hope you are taking opportunities to surf the Net. You won't be able to understand how consumers use the Web unless you do it yourself.

If you have surfed the Web, maybe you've had a few experiences like this: you set out with a list of things to look for and routes to take ("Let's try WebCrawler here and see what they have for Boston") and ten minutes later, by a process impossible to describe, you find yourself reading a list of "24 Hawaiian canoe plants." That's right, canoe plants. Whatever happened to Boston? "Okay, this time let's go back to Yahoo and try Boston again."

The Web is like that. It is an ever-changing kaleidoscope of potential distractions, surprises and opportunities. The customers you are seeking here are comfortable wandering around discovering things for themselves on the Net.

Some real estate agents find it unnerving that such cyber-window-shopping goes on 24 hours a day with no live agent there to control the outcome. Instead of lingering glumly behind while potential buyers and sellers explore markets without you, catch up and stroll along with them. If you are going to open your own "store" on the World Wide Web, you need to do some surfing, too.

Glossary

anonymous FTP
A site that lets you log on without a secret password and lets you move files between that computer and yours.

application
(a) Software that performs a particular useful function for you. ("Do you have an electronic mail application installed on your computer?")
(b) The useful function itself (e.g., transferring files is a useful application of the Internet).

ARPAnet
An experimental network established in the 1970s where the theories and software on which the Internet is based were tested. No longer in existence.

bandwidth
The size of a network and its ability to carry data. The more bandwidth or larger the network, the more data that can go through the network at once.

baud
When transmitting data, the number of times the medium's "state" changes per second. For example: a 2400-baud modem changes the signal it sends on the phone line 2400 times per second. Since each change in state can correspond to multiple bits of data, the actual bit rate of data transfer may exceed the baud rate. Also see "bits per second."

BBS (Bulletin Board System)
Used in networking to refer to a system for providing online announcements, with or without provisions for user input. Internet hosts often provide them in addition to Usenet conferences.

beta
A test version of a software application.

bits per second
The speed at which bits are transmitted over a communications medium.

bridge

Hardware used to expand the capability of a LAN by selectively forwarding information to another part of the LAN.

BTW

Common abbreviation in mail and news, meaning "by the way."

Chat (Internet Relay Chat or IRC)

A service that allows large group conversations over the Internet.

client

A software application (q.v.) that works on your behalf to extract a service from a server somewhere on the network. Think of your telephone as a client and the telephone company as a server to get the idea.

CMA

Comparative Market Analysis

commercial networks or service providers

Companies such as America Online, Prodigy, and CompuServe support private networks. Many of these networks now provide access to the Internet in addition to their own content. Because of their additional content and ease of use, they are often more expensive than going to an ISP.

CRS

Certified Residential Specialist

dial-up access

A type of connection to the Internet that allows you to call a computer directly on the Internet, staying connected only during the time you are online. Dial-up access is cheaper, but slower than direct access.

direct access

A permanent connection to the Internet that continues even if you are away from your computer. Direct access is faster and more expensive than dial-up access.

distribution list

A mailing list that sends out a newsletter or bulletin to its subscribers. This may be the list's sole purpose.

DNS (Domain Name System)

A distributed database system for translating computer names (like *ruby.ora.com*) into numeric Internet addresses (like 194.56.78.2), and vice versa. DNS allows you to use the Internet without remembering long lists of numbers.

download

To move a file from a remote computer or server onto yours.

email

One of the most popular tools on the Internet. With email software, you can send messages, documents, and graphics to other people connected to the Internet.

Ethernet

A kind of local area network. There are several different kinds of wiring, which support different communication speeds, ranging from 2 to 10 million bits per second. What makes an Ethernet an Ethernet is the way the computers on the network decide whose turn it is to talk. Computers using TCP/IP are frequently connected to the Internet over an Ethernet.

FAQ (Frequently Asked Questions)

Either a frequently asked question, or a list of frequently asked questions and their answers. Many Usenet newsgroups, and some non-Usenet mailing lists, maintain FAQ lists (FAQs) so that participants don't spend time answering the same set of questions. (Pronounced "fack" or spelled out F-A-Q.)

firewall

A software program on a host computer that blocks access to unauthorized entry.

flame

A virulent and (often) largely personal attack against the author of a Usenet posting. Flames are unfortunately common. People who frequently write flames are known as "flamers."

frame relay

A data communication technology which is sometimes used to provide higher speed (above 56 Kb and less than 1.5 Mb) for Internet connections. Its usual application is in connecting work groups rather than individuals.

Freenet

An organization providing free Internet access to people in a certain area, usually through public libraries.

FSBO

For Sale By Owner

FTP

(a) The File Transfer Protocol; a protocol that defines how to transfer files from one computer to another.

(b) An application program that moves files using the File Transfer Protocol.

FYI

A common abbreviation in mail and news, meaning "for your information."

gateway

A computer system that transfers data between normally incompatible applications or networks. It reformats the data so that it is acceptable for the new network (or application) before passing it on. A gateway might connect two dissimilar networks, like DECnet and the Internet, or it might allow two incompatible applications to communicate over the same network (like mail systems with different message formats). The term is often used interchangeably with router (q.v.), but this usage is incorrect.

GIF (Graphical Interchange Format)

Developed by CompuServe online services, this graphic file format allows images to transfer over telephone lines more quickly than other graphic formats.

Gopher

A menu-based system for exploring Internet resources.

GRI

Graduate Realtors Institute

hit

The number of times someone accesses a Web site.

home page

The introductory page to a Web site. You may start with this page or you may start elsewhere on the Web site depending on how you entered.

hostname

That portion of a URL that defines who the host is, i.e., *ibm.com* or *apple.com.*

hotlink

A color-coded portion of text displayed on a Web site that, if clicked on, takes you to another site or document.

HTML (HyperText Markup Language)

The language in which World Wide Web documents are written.

HTTP (HyperText Transfer Protocol)

The language computers speak to each other to transfer World Wide Web data.

hypermedia

A combination of hypertext (q.v.) and multimedia (q.v.).

hypertext

Documents that contain links to other documents; selecting a link automatically displays the second document.

IAB (Internet Architecture Board)

The "ruling council" that makes decisions about standards and other important issues.

IETF (Internet Engineering Task Force)

A volunteer group that investigates and solves technical problems and makes recommendations to the IAB (q.v.).

image

A picture or graphic that appears on a Web page.

IMHO

Common abbreviation in mail and news, meaning "in my humble opinion."

Internet (or Net)

(a)   Generally (not capitalized), any collection of distinct networks working together as one.

(b)   Specifically (capitalized), the worldwide "network of networks" that are connected to each other, using IP and other similar protocols. The Internet provides file transfer, remote login, electronic mail, news, and other services.

intranet

Private portions of the Internet set up mostly by companies that want to use the powerful networking features of the Net for their own company networking purposes.

IP (Internet Protocol)

The most important of the protocols on which the Internet is based. It allows a packet to traverse multiple networks on the way to its final destination.

IRC

See Chat

ISDN (Integrated Services Digital Network)

A digital telephone service. With ISDN service, phone lines carry digital signals, rather than analog signals. If you have the appropriate hardware and software, if your local central office provides ISDN service, and if your service provider supports it, ISDN allows high-speed home or office access to the Internet (56 Kb).

ISOC (Internet Society)

An organization whose members support a worldwide information network. It is also the governing body to which the IAB (q.v.) reports.

ISP (Internet Service Provider)

An organization that supplies users with access to the Internet.

Java
A program produced by Sun Microsystems that allows for a higher degree of interactivity, motion, and sound on Web pages.

jpeg/jpg
A graphic (pictures) format that compresses an image and makes it easier to transmit.

keyword search
An electronic search that allows you to find more information than a subject search because the computer looks at words in the titles and content of a source as well as the subjects. It also allows you to find more specific information, because each source yields many more keywords than subjects. The challenge in using keyword searching is to refine your topic so that the search yields an adequate number of useful citations.

kill file
A list of newsgroup users whose postings you do not want to read. You can create a kill file and include email addresses of people whose messages you don't wish to read.

LAN (local area network)
A network that connects computers and other peripherals in a small area, such as a building or classroom.

leased line
A permanently connected private telephone line between two locations. Leased lines are typically used to connect a moderate-sized local network to an Internet Service Provider.

link
The text or graphic you click on to make a hypertext jump to another page.

listserv
See mailing list

mailing list
A conference/discussion group on a specific topic where all messages are sent to one email address and then redistributed to the email boxes of the list's subscribers. If the list is moderated, someone will review the messages before redistributing them.

MLS
Multiple Listing Service

modem
A piece of equipment that connects a computer to a data transmission line (typically a telephone line of some sort). Most people use modems that transfer data at speeds ranging from 1200 bits per second (bps) to

19.2 Kbps. There are also modems providing higher speeds and supporting other media. These are used for special purposes, for example, to connect a large local network to its network provider over a leased line.

moderated

A newsgroup or mailing list that has a person screening the messages coming in before he or she posts them to subscribers.

Mosaic

One particular browser for the World Wide Web; supports hypermedia. Mosaic is often used (incorrectly) as a synonym for the World Wide Web.

multimedia

Documents that include different kinds of data; for example, plain text and audio, text in several different languages, or plain text and a spreadsheet.

Netscape

The most well-known and commonly used browser; many people use "Netscape" as a generic term to refer to the Web or to browsers in general.

newbie

You, maybe. A newcomer to the Internet.

newsgroup

A conference/discussion group where people post and read messages at the newsgroup site rather than in a mailbox. Reading the messages requires your ISP to subscribe to the newsgroup and for you to use a newsreader. Newsgroups are organized by subject area (i.e., *need a newsgroup here*)

newsreader

A software program that allows you to read and post messages to newsgroups.

packet

A bundle of data. On the Internet, data is broken up into small chunks, called packets; each packet traverses the network independently. Packet sizes can vary from roughly 40 to 32,000 bytes, depending on network hardware and media, but packets are normally less than 1500 bytes long.

port

(a) A number that identifies a particular Internet application. When your computer sends a packet to another computer, that packet contains information about what protocol it's using (e.g., TCP or UDP), and what application it's trying to communicate with. The port number identifies the application.

(b) One of a computer's physical input/output channels (i.e., a plug on the back of the computer).

Unfortunately, these two meanings are completely unrelated. The first is more common when you're talking about the Internet (as in "Telnet to port

1000"); the second is more common when you're talking about hardware ("connect your modem to the serial port on the back of your computer").

post

An individual article sent to a Usenet (q.v.) newsgroup, or the act of sending an article to a Usenet newsgroup.

PPP (Point-to-Point Protocol)

A protocol that allows a computer to use the TCP/IP (Internet) protocols (and become a full-fledged Internet member) with a standard telephone line and a high-speed modem. PPP is a new standard, which replaces SLIP (q.v.). Although PPP is less common than SLIP, it's quickly increasing in popularity.

protocol

A definition of how computers will act when talking to each other. Protocol definitions range from how bits are placed on a wire to the format of an electronic mail message. Standard protocols allow computers from different manufacturers to communicate; the computers can use completely different software, providing that the programs running on both ends agree on what the data means.

Real Estate Settlement Procedures Act (RESPA)

Federal regulations that limit what kinds of fees agents can receive for arranging real estate financing and other services for homebuyers.

real time

Synchronous communication. For example, talking to someone on the phone is in real time, whereas listening to a message someone left on your answering machine is not (asynchronous communication).

REIT

Real Estate Investment Trust

REO

Real Estate Owned (or repossessed by the lender)

router

A system that transfers data between two or more networks using the same protocols. The networks may differ in physical characteristics (e.g., a router may transfer data between an Ethernet and a leased telephone line).

scanner

A piece of computer equipment that converts photos and other hardcopy into graphic computer files.

search engine

A Web-based tool that finds Web pages based on terms and criteria specified.

server

(a) Software that allows a computer to offer a service to another computer. Other computers contact the server program by means of matching client (q.v.) software.

(b) The computer on which the server software runs.

service provider

An organization that provides connections to a part of the Internet. If you want to connect your company's network or your personal computer to the Internet, you have to talk to a service provider.

shareware

Software made available, usually over the Internet, for free on a trial basis. The developer asks those who keep and use it to pay a nominal fee.

shell

On a UNIX system, software that accepts and processes command lines from your terminal. UNIX has multiple shells available (e.g., C shell, Bourne shell, Korn shell), each with slightly different command formats and facilities.

signature

A file, typically about five lines long, that people often insert at the end of electronic mail messages or Usenet news articles. A signature contains, minimally, a name and an email address. Signatures usually also contain postal addresses, and often contain silly quotes, pictures, and other things. Some are elaborate, though signatures more than five or six lines long are in questionable taste.

SLIP (Serial Line Internet Protocol)

A protocol that allows a computer to use the Internet protocols (and become a full-fledged Internet member) with a standard telephone line and a high-speed modem. SLIP is being superseded by PPP (q.v.), but is still in common use.

smiley

Smiling faces used in mail and news to indicate humor and irony. The most common smiley is :-). You'll also see :-(meaning disappointment, and lots of other variations.

snail mail

Mail sent via the post office or express delivery service.

spamming

The frowned-upon practice of sending large amounts of junk email to people who have not requested it.

subject search

An electronic search based on the traditional method of categorizing books and other materials by subject. These subjects are usually fairly broad general topics established by an authority such as the Library of Congress.

subscribe

Joining a mailing list or newsgroup to read and send message to the group.

surf

To mindlessly click from link to link on the Internet looking for something interesting.

TCP (Transmission Control Protocol)

One of the protocols on which the Internet is based. TCP is a connection-oriented reliable protocol.

telecommuting

Pretending you're working at home.

Telnet

(a) A terminal emulation protocol that allows you to log in to other computer systems on the Internet.

(b) An application program that allows you to log in to another computer system using the protocol.

tiff file

Another graphic format for pictures.

timeout

What happens when two computers are talking and one computer, for any reason, fails to respond. The other computer will keep on trying for a certain amount of time, but will eventually give up.

UNIX

A popular operating system that was very important in the development of the Internet. Contrary to rumor, though, you do *not* have to use UNIX to use the Internet. There are various flavors of UNIX. Two common ones are BSD and System V.

upload

To move a file from your computer to another computer or server.

URL (Universal Resource Locator)

The combination of letters and numbers that uniquely identifies a Web resource.

Usenet

An informal, rather anarchic, group of systems that exchange news. News is essentially similar to bulletin boards on other networks. Usenet actually predates the Internet, but these days, the Internet is used to transfer much of the Usenet's traffic.

username

The name you receive from your service provider to identify your account on the host computer. Generally, your user name is created from your real name, such as your first name and last initial. Your user name is to the left of the @ symbol in your email address.

value-added network (VAN)

A computer network that groups related businesses so they can provide their customers with a one-stop service. For example, a real estate VAN would include real estate offices, title and insurance companies, pest control firms, and lenders.

WAIS (Wide Area Information Service)

A powerful system for looking up information in databases or libraries across the Internet.

Web

See World Wide Web

Web browser

A software program that allows you to view, search, and download items from the Web. Common browsers are Netscape and Mosaic.

Web page

A file accessible by a Web browser. Web pages can contain text, sounds, pictures, movies, and hypertext links to other Web pages.

Web server

A computer directly connected to the Internet that responds to requests from browsers to send Web pages.

Web site

A set of Web pages for a person or organization.

Webmaster

A person who maintains a Web site.

World Wide Web

A hypertext-based system for finding and accessing Internet resources. Also known as WWW or the Web.

WWW

See World Wide Web

Index

sh**o**p**PBS**

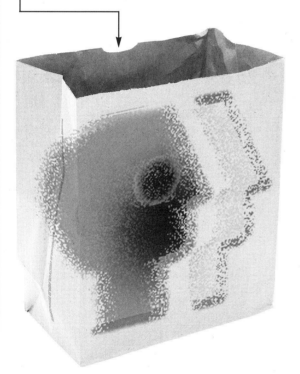

from the comfort of your own computer chair

What is shopPBS? It's the latest innovation from PBS ONLINE that literally puts the power to obtain PBS's renowned videos and products at your fingertips.

More than 190 series and individual program videos, a colorful PBS ONLINE t-shirt, the acclaimed book *NetLearning: How Teachers Use the Internet,* and the lovable Wishbone doll are some of the many items available for purchase at this special cyber store. Best of all, ordering is done online with secure transactions!

For a fun-filled adventure, make your next online stop shopPBS at *http://www.pbs.org/shop.*

PBS ONLINE® (http://www.pbs.org) is the premier choice for unique and compelling interactive content developed specifically for the Internet.

INTERNET PRODUCTS

Summer 1996

WebSite™ 1.1

By O'Reilly & Associates, Inc.
Documentation by Susan Peck & Stephen Arrants
2nd Edition January 1996
Four diskettes, 494-pg book, WebSite T-shirt
ISBN 1-56592-173-9; UPC 9-781565-921733
Upgrade offer from Website 1.0 available

Introducing the latest version of our award-winning *WebSite™*, a 32-bit multi-threaded World Wide Web server for Windows NT ™3.5 or higher and Windows®95. *WebSite* is the elegant and easy solution for anyone who wants to publish information on the Internet or on a corporate LAN.

The *WebSite* server lets you maintain a set of Web documents, control access, index desktop directories, and use a CGI program to display data from applications such as Excel®, Access™, Visual Basic, and other programs. *WebSite* includes WebView™, a powerful Web management tool that provides a tree-like display of all documents and links on your server, logging statistics, and searching and indexing features. It also includes the new Spyglass Mosaic™ 2.1 Web browser and full online Help, as well as a *WebSite* book, which has won rave reviews from users and the press.

New version 1.1 features include the HotDog™ Standard HTML editor which supports text formatting, link building, tables, and forms; WebView printing, so you can print a view of your Web contents; a new graphical interface for creating virtual servers; enhanced search capabilities; server side includes (SSI), to combine static and programmed documents on the fly; and a Visual Basic 4 framework with sample applications, which significantly improves the speed and efficiency of working with spreadsheets, databases, and other programs.

"*WebSite* is a developer's dream, offering a full set of tools and examples in interactively extending the Web server. And it includes enough Web-management tools to keep even the fussiest Webmaster satisfied.... *WebSite* gives you much for your money: great documentation, lots of sample CGI scripts, and a noteworthy organizational viewer."
—Kevin Reichard, *PC Magazine*

WebSite Professional™

By O'Reilly & Associates, Inc.
Documentation by Susan Peck
1st Edition Summer 1996
Includes 3 books
ISBN 1-56592-174-7; UPC 9-781565-921740

Designed for the sophisticated user, *WebSite Professional™* is a complete Web server solution. *WebSite Professional* contains all of *WebSite*'s award-winning features, including remote administration, virtual servers for creating multiple home pages, wizards to automate common tasks, a search tool for Web indexing, and a graphical outline for Web documents and links for managing your site. New with *WebSite Professional*: support for SSL and S-HTTP, the premier Web encryption security protocols; the WebSite Application Programming Interface (WSAPI); Cold Fusion™, and support for client and server-side Java programming.

WebSite Professional is a must for sophisticated users who want to offer their audiences the best in Web server technology.

Summary of *WebSite Professional* features:

- Provides a complete Web server security solution that includes digital signatures and privacy for the exchange of payment information, personal identification, and intellectual property.

- Supports the two major cryptographic security systems, Secure Sockets Layer (SSL) and Secure Hypertext Transfer Protocol (S-HTTP). SSL security applies to network connections; S-HTTP security applies to documents. *WebSite Professional* has an easy interface for S-HTTP administration through WebView.

- New WebSite Application Programming Interface (WSAPI) with enhanced logging, post processing, document genera tion, authentication, and other features.

- Cold Fusion™, a powerful database application development tool for easily incorporating database information into your Web documents. Cold Fusion lets you quickly develop applications to add customer feedback, online ordering, event registration, interactive training, online technical support, and more to your site.

For information: **800-998-9938**, 707-829-0515; **info@ora.com; http://www.ora.com/**
To order: **800-889-8969** (credit card orders only); **order@ora.com**

S T U D I O S

Songline Studios specializes in developing innovative, interactive content for online audiences.

Songline Studios mission is to create online programs that allow audiences to experience new people, places, and ideas in unique ways that can only be accomplished through the Web. "Users are not just looking for information online but are searching for rewarding experiences. We are focused on creating these experiences," notes Dale Dougherty, president and CEO of Songline Studios.

THE MEANING OF "SONGLINE"

Songline Studios derives its name from the Australian aboriginal concept of using songs to guide people through unknown territories. These oral maps or "songlines" depict events at successive sites along a walking trail that traverses through a region. This is evocative of Songline Studios' mission: to create resources and guides for online audiences as they seek out and experience new territories and new communities on the Internet.

You can visit the many online and print properties created by Songline Studios through their Web site located at *http://www.songline.com*

SONGLINE GUIDES

The Songline Guides book series connects people with their communities of interest on the Internet. They are non-technical guides, featuring the experiences of specific community members who are also early Internet adopters. These stories help the reader focus on what he or she might expect to gain from being online. Songline Guides can be found at your local bookstore or can be ordered directly from O'Reilly & Associates by calling **1-800-998-9938** or send an email message to **order@ora.com**. Look for Songline Guides for Realtors, Parents and other communities of interest in the near future.

**For more information about Songline Studios, call 1-800-998-9973
or send email to: *info@songline.com***

Stay in touch with O'REILLY™

Visit Our Award-Winning World Wide Web Site

http://www.ora.com

VOTED

"Top 100 Sites on the Web" —*PC Magazine*
"Top 5% Websites" —*Point Communications*
"3-Star site" —*The McKinley Group*

Our Web site contains a library of comprehensive product information (including book excerpts and tables of contents), downloadable software, background articles, interviews with technology leaders, links to relevant sites, book cover art, and more. File us in your Bookmarks or Hotlist!

Join Our Two Email Mailing Lists

LIST #1   NEW PRODUCT RELEASES: To receive automatic email with brief descriptions of all new O'Reilly products as they are released, send email to: listproc@online.ora.com and put the following information in the first line of your message (NOT in the Subject: field, which is ignored):
**subscribe ora-news "Your Name"
of "Your Organization"**
(for example: **subscribe ora-news
Kris Webber of Fine Enterprises)**

List #2   O'REILLY EVENTS: If you'd also like us to send information about trade show events, special promotions, and other O'Reilly events, send email to: **listproc@online.ora.com** and put the following information in the first line of your message (NOT in the Subject: field, which is ignored): **subscribe ora-events
"Your Name" of "Your Organization"**

Visit Our Gopher Site

- Connect your Gopher to **gopher.ora.com**, or
- Point your Web browser to **gopher://gopher.ora.com/**, or
- telnet to **gopher.ora.com** (login: **gopher**)

Get Example Files from Our Books Via FTP

There are two ways to access an archive of example files from our books:

REGULAR FTP — ftp to: **ftp.ora.com**
(login: **anonymous**—use your email address as the password) or point your Web browser to: **ftp://ftp.ora.com/**

FTPMAIL — Send an email message to: **ftpmail@online.ora.com** (write "help" in the message body)

Contact Us Via Email

order@ora.com — To place a book or software order online. Good for North American and international customers.

subscriptions@ora.com — To place an order for any of our newsletters or periodicals.

software@ora.com — For general questions and product information about our software.
 • Check out O'Reilly Software Online at **http://software.ora.com** for software and technical support information.
 • Registered O'Reilly software users send your questions to **website-support@ora.com**

books@ora.com — General questions about any of our books.

cs@ora.com — For answers to problems regarding your order or our product.

booktech@ora.com — For book content technical questions or corrections.

proposals@ora.com — To submit new book or software proposals to our editors and product managers.

international@ora.com — For information about our international distributors or translation queries
 • For a list of our distributors outside of North America check out: **http://www.ora.com/www/order/country.html**

O'REILLY™

101 Morris Street, Sebastopol, CA 95472 USA
TEL 707-829-0515 or 800-998-9938 (6 A.M. to 5 P.M. PST)
FAX 707-829-0104

International Distributors

Customers outside North America can now order O'Reilly & Associates books through the following distributors. They offer our international customers faster order processing, more bookstores, increased representation at tradeshowsworldwide, and the high-quality, responsive service our customers have come to expect.

EUROPE, MIDDLE EAST AND NORTHERN AFRICA (EXCEPT GERMANY, SWITZERLAND, AND AUSTRIA)

INQUIRIES

International Thomson Publishing Europe
Berkshire House
168-173 High Holborn
London WC1V 7AA, United Kingdom
Telephone: 44-171-497-1422
Fax: 44-171-497-1426
Email: itpint@itps.co.uk

ORDERS

International Thomson Publishing Services, Ltd.
Cheriton House, North Way
Andover, Hampshire SP10 5BE,
United Kingdom
Telephone: 44-264-342-832 (UK orders)
Telephone: 44-264-342-806 (outside UK)
Fax: 44-264-364418 (UK orders)
Fax: 44-264-342761 (outside UK)
UK & Eire orders: itpuk@itps.co.uk
International orders: itpint@itps.co.uk

GERMANY, SWITZERLAND, AND AUSTRIA

International Thomson Publishing GmbH
O'Reilly International Thomson Verlag
Königswinterer Straße 418
53227 Bonn, Germany
Telephone: 49-228-97024 0
Fax: 49-228-441342
Email: anfragen@arade.ora.de

AUSTRALIA

WoodsLane Pty. Ltd.
7/5 Vuko Place, Warriewood NSW 2102
P.O. Box 935, Mona Vale NSW 2103
Australia
Telephone: 61-2-9970-5111
Fax: 61-2-9970-5002
Email: info@woodslane.com.au

NEW ZEALAND

WoodsLane New Zealand Ltd.
21 Cooks Street (P.O. Box 575)
Wanganui, New Zealand
Telephone: 64-6-347-6543
Fax: 64-6-345-4840
Email: woods@tmx.mhs.oz.au

ASIA *(except Japan & India)*

INQUIRIES

International Thomson Publishing Asia
60 Albert Street #15-01
Albert Complex
Singapore 189969
Telephone: 65-336-6411
Fax: 65-336-7411

ORDERS

Telephone: 65-336-6411
Fax: 65-334-1617

JAPAN

O'Reilly Japan, Inc.
Kiyoshige Building 2F
12-Banchi, Sanei-cho
Shinjuku-ku
Tokyo 160 Japan
Telephone: 8-3-3356-55227
Fax: 81-3-3356-5261
Email: kenj@ora.com

INDIA

Computer Bookshop (India) PVT. LTD.
190 Dr. D.N. Road, Fort
Bombay 400 001
India
Telephone: 91-22-207-0989
Fax: 91-22-262-3551
Email: cbsbom@giasbm01.vsnl.net.in

THE AMERICAS

O'Reilly & Associates, Inc.
101 Morris Street
Sebastopol, CA 95472 U.S.A.
Telephone: 707-829-0515
Telephone: 800-998-9938 (U.S. & Canada)
Fax: 707-829-0104
Email: order@ora.com

SOUTHERN AFRICA

International Thomson Publishing Southern Africa
Building 18, Constantia Park
240 Old Pretoria Road
P.O. Box 2459
Halfway House, 1685 South Africa
Telephone: 27-11-805-4819
Fax: 27-11-805-3648

 *NetSuccess: How Real Estate Agents Use the Internet* includes the GNN Internet service and GNNpress for Windows 95 on the enclosed CD-ROM. The GNN Internet service gives you full Internet connectivity plus GNN content. GNNpress is a Web authoring tool that allows GNN members to create their own Web sites quickly and easily.

GNN does provide its own Web browser, but you can use others, such as Netscape, if you prefer. You can download the Netscape browser by pointing the GNN Web browser to *http://home.netscape.com/comprod/mirror/client_download.html*

A Macintosh version of the GNN service and GNNpress with a customized Netscape browser will be available at a later time. Contact 1-800-819-6112 for more information.

Here's a page we encourage readers to tear out...

SONGLINE™
S T U D I O S

O'REILLY WOULD LIKE TO HEAR FROM YOU

Which book did this card come from?

_____

Where did you buy this book?
- ❑ Bookstore
- ❑ Direct from O'Reilly
- ❑ Bundled with hardware/software
- ❑ Other _____
- ❑ Computer Store
- ❑ Class/seminar

What operating system do you use?
- ❑ UNIX
- ❑ Windows NT
- ❑ Other _____
- ❑ Macintosh
- ❑ PC(Windows/DOS)

What is your job description?
- ❑ System Administrator
- ❑ Network Administrator
- ❑ Web Developer
- ❑ Other _____
- ❑ Programmer
- ❑ Educator/Teacher

❑ Please send me *ora.com*, O'Reilly's catalog, containing a complete listing of O'Reilly books and software.

Name _____ Company/Organization _____

Address _____

City _____ State _____ Zip/Postal Code _____ Country _____

Telephone _____ Internet or other email address (specify network) _____

Songline Studios specializes in
developing innovative, interactive
content for online audiences. Visit
the many online and print properties created by Songline Studios
through their Website located at
http://www.songline.com

Songline Inc., 101 Morris Street, Sebastopol, CA 95472-9902

BUSINESS REPLY MAIL
FIRST CLASS MAIL   PERMIT NO. 80   SEBASTOPOL, CA

Postage will be paid by addressee

O'Reilly & Associates, Inc.
101 Morris Street
Sebastopol, CA 95472-9902